T0330107

MARKET CAPITALISM AND MORAL VALUES

The Section F Series
British Association for the Advancement of Science

Market Capitalism and Moral Values

Proceedings of Section F (Economics) of the
British Association for the Advancement of Science
Keele 1993

Edited by
Samuel Brittan and Alan Hamlin

Edward Elgar

Published by
Edward Elgar Publishing Limited
Gower House
Croft Road
Aldershot
Hants GU11 3HR
England

Edward Elgar Publishing Company
Old Post Road
Brookfield
Vermont 05036
USA

British Library Cataloguing in Publication Data
Market Capitalism and Moral Values:
Proceedings of Section F (Economics) of
the British Association for the
Advancement of Science, Keele, 1993
   I. Brittan, Samuel II. Hamlin, Alan P.
   33.01

Library of Congress Cataloguing in Publication Data
British Association for the Advancement of Science. Section F
   (Economics). Meeting (1993: Keele, Staffordshire)
     Market capitalism and moral values: proceedings of Section F
   (Economics) of the British Association for the Advancement of
   Science, Keele, 1993 / edited by Samuel Brittan & Alan Hamlin
      p.   cm.
     1. Economics—Moral and ethical aspects—Congresses.
   2. Capitalism—Moral and ethical aspects—Congresses. I. Brittan,
   Samuel. II. Hamlin, Alan P., 1951– . III. Title.
   HB72.B74 1993
   330—dc20   94–29160
                                                           CIP

ISBN 1 85898 080 1

Printed and bound in Great Britain by
Biddles Limited, Guildford and King's Lynn

Contents

List of figures   vii
List of contributors   ix
Introduction   xi

1 Economics and ethics   1
   Samuel Brittan
2 Moral codes and economic success   23
   Amartya Sen
3 Some reflections on morality and capitalism   35
   Nigel Lawson
4 The ethics of unemployment and Mafia capitalism   45
   John S. Flemming
5 What moral constraints for business?   57
   Norman Barry
6 Fairness in the rationing of health care   79
   John Broome
7 The role of ethics in Keynes's economics   88
   Robert Skidelsky
8 Ethical constraints on price flexibility   101
   Massimo M. Beber and Lorenzo Ornaghi
9 Altruism, ethics and economics: the significance of non-egoistic
   preferences for economics   120
   John Fender
10 The moral of the market   137
   Alan Hamlin

Index   151

Figures

1.1	Co-operation and confession	10
9.1	The prisoner's dilemma	123
9.2	Taxation and the prisoner's dilemma	124
9.3	Altruism and the prisoner's dilemma	125
9.4	The altruist's dilemma	128
9.5	A co-ordination game	133

List of contributors

Norman Barry   Professor of Politics at the University of Buckingham.

Massimo M. Beber   Fellow of Selwyn College, Cambridge.

John Broome   Professor of Economics and Ethics at the University of Bristol.

Samuel Brittan   President of Section F of the British Association for the Advancement of Science and Assistant Editor of the *Financial Times*.

John Fender   Senior Lecturer in Economics at the University of Birmingham.

John S. Flemming   Warden of Wadham College, Oxford and formerly Chief Economist of The European Bank for Reconstruction and Development.

Alan Hamlin   Reader in Economics at the University of Southampton.

Nigel Lawson   Lord Lawson, Conservative MP from 1974 to 1992, and Chancellor of the Exchequer from 1983 to 1989.

Lorenzo Ornaghi   Professor of Political Science at the Catholic University of the Sacred Heart, Milan.

Amartya Sen   Lamont University Professor and Professor of Economics and Philosophy, Harvard University.

Robert Skidelsky   Lord Skidelsky, Professor of Political Economy at the University of Warwick.

Introduction

Men and women do not live by self-interest alone. They are constrained in its pursuit by rules, conventions and beliefs, even if they are far from saints. Hence the saying that there is honour among thieves.

My main concern in suggesting 'economics and ethics' for the theme of Section F (Economics) at the 1993 annual meeting of the British Association for the Advancement of Science was to examine the effects of different moral beliefs on the operation of markets. In my invitation to speakers I wrote:

> The emphasis is not intended to be on the ethical evaluation of economic systems or ideas. It is meant to be the other way round: the effect of moral beliefs on economic conduct.
>
> Most economists assume that economic agents maximize utility subject to constraints. The key constraints are often not just those of limited budgets, or even the physical and institutional environment, but beliefs and moral codes. For example the degree of wage and price flexibility is dependent *inter alia* on beliefs about the acceptability of undercutting or pricing into work.
>
> Speakers are, of course, free to interpret the theme in their own way and they can adopt a positive or normative approach, or a mixture of both. The analysis of the effects of beliefs may lead speakers to ideas on institutions and policies, or even on the suitability or otherwise of widespread ethical norms.

As the wording of the last paragraph shows, I realized that the positive evaluation of the effects of moral beliefs on the working of markets was too new a field to occupy the attention of all the speakers, and that there was still something to say in the older debate on the morality of market capitalism. The newer subject matter was, however, analysed by several contributors.

As the reader will realize from the contents list, there was an extremely good response, both from renowned authorities and from younger scholars; and the informal interchange of ideas, which is so important a part of these gatherings, was enjoyable and fruitful.

Thanks are due to many people and, as a newcomer to the British Association, I am bound to omit some. T. Rybczinski contributed the same unfailing enthusiasm which has sustained Section F over many years. The Section's treasurer, Alan Winters, was an unfailing source of guidance whose careful husbanding of resources has enabled the meetings to continue from year to year without a break. Anne Milson and Sue Lowell of the Association went beyond their normal duties in helping with the administration in a time of crisis. The University of Keele provided a most congenial setting for our activities. Here thanks are due to John Proops, the local organizer of Section F, who made the whole event come together.

Special thanks are due to three people. Douglas Mair, an outstanding former recorder, kindly agreed to return as acting recorder. Whether or not there is no such thing as society, there would have been no such thing as Section F in 1993 without Mair. Alan Hamlin undertook at short notice the arduous job of editing and processing the conference papers into this volume. In addition, he has written a model concluding analytical assessment which should help any perplexed reader to find his way through the preceding papers. Above all, he has suggested criteria by which rival claims can be put to the test. Finally the publisher, Edward Elgar, has exerted himself in helping and encouraging the conference volume in a way which itself falsifies any assumption of narrow self-interest.

Samuel Brittan
London

1 Economics and ethics
Samuel Brittan

Introduction

A well-known and fair-minded television commentator stated that he found it odd to begin a television series on the background to the conflict and misery in Bosnia with 'a lecture by currency manipulator George Soros, of all people, on ethics'.

The commentator in question, Christopher Dunkley, immediately qualified his observation by reminding us that Soros had in fact 'spent some of the millions he had made in speculating against the pound on liberal and humane charities in the area in question'. He added that the content of Soros's lecture 'on the need for a new world order based on the Open Society...where minorities and minority opinion are respected' was 'wholly laudable'.

But the impression remained that, however praiseworthy the financier's other actions, these were an offset to immoral professional behaviour. As against this was the view, particularly widespread in the English language anti-EC media, that speculators deserved a medal for helping to bring down unrealistic currency parities and systems.

I start with an unresolved headline issue to make the simple point that the relationship between moral evaluation and economic analysis has come back into fashion. It went underground in the heyday of the belief in economics as a supposedly technical guide to action; but it has now resurfaced.

A sign of the times in the academic sphere is that the lead article in the June 1993 issue of *The Journal of Economic Literature* is entitled 'Economics and Contemporary Moral Philosophy'. The authors consider the relationship important for four reasons (I have changed the order):

1. Some moral commitments are necessary to evaluate either whole economic systems or more limited policy proposals.
2. The study of positive economics – of what is – turns out to be extremely difficult to separate from normative economics – of what should be – for reasons that go deep into the structure of human language and action.
3. The highly technical subject known as 'welfare economics' – which is only remotely connected with the welfare state – rests on complex and disputable moral presuppositions.
4. The moral beliefs of economic agents influence their behaviour in the market-place.

It is on the last of these aspects that I wish to concentrate, even though it has received the least academic study.

One reason why the whole subject was for so long underemphasized was a little bit of what I can only call economists' do-it-yourself philosophy. This is the prejudice that it is impossible to have a reasoned discussion of alternative ends, because such a discussion would depend on value judgements which are supposed to be a pure matter of personal taste: so that disapproval of disparities of income and wealth is regarded as like a taste for strawberry ice-cream, about which no argument is possible.

People can and do argue about moral beliefs without violating Hume's law that you cannot derive an 'ought' from an 'is' statement. If the consequences of holding beliefs play any part in your moral outlook, then you should be prepared to modify your beliefs in relation to what you discover these consequences to be.

Perhaps the best way of demonstrating how this can be done is still Sen's distinction in *Collective Choice and Social Welfare* between a basic and a non-basic value judgement. A basic judgement is one that applies in all conceivable circumstances. If circumstances can be envisaged where a judgement would not apply, it is non-basic. Take the statement, 'men and women should be allowed to dress as they like'. This may appear to be an ultra-liberal, but undiscussable, basic judgement. Suppose, however, that the person who utters it flinches when asked if he or she would still hold to it, even if it turned out that mini-skirts cause cancer in the eye of the beholder. In that case, the judgement turns out to be non-basic. The fundamental point is that there is no way of demonstrating in advance that a judgement is basic, as no one would have occasion to consider all conceivable circumstances in forming a judgement. Where we have not had to face a concrete choice we may simply not know what our real values are.

The post-communist world
The importance of the moral aspects of economics should have been brought home by the events in the former communist countries, and especially the former Soviet Union. More thoughtful economists have always known that markets need a background not only of formal laws, but also of accepted rules of behaviour, if the 'invisible hand' is to work.

Unfortunately, the content of these rules has been taken for granted rather than studied by most mainstream economists. The influence of beliefs on behaviour has been confined to discussions over coffee, and their study left to sociologists and others, often unsympathetic to the market process. Yet it is just this aspect, which economists have neglected in their formal work – such as the domain of permissible actions which can be taken against competitors, or the rules and conventions governing private and state property – which have proved crucial in Russia and its neighbours, rather than the theorems which have been the predominant study of high-level professional economists. The most important understanding needed in the newly emerging market economies is not of refinements of marginal cost pricing in or out of general equilibria, but of the difference between criminal behaviour and legitimate profit-seeking.

The need is for an empirically grounded study of how market institutions are built up from the Hobbesian 'war of all against all' which otherwise emerges from the destruction of a central dictatorship. So-called soft subjects, such as cultural history, may have more to tell us about the different outcomes of the breakdown of central planning in the Czech Republic, Russia, the outlying former Soviet republics and China, than mainstream economics.

Immoral morality

An extremely important point to clarify is that the influence of moral beliefs is not necessarily for the good. This statement is not self-contradictory, so long as we use the word 'moral' to describe beliefs to which we are not necessarily committed ourselves. The alternative usage, which is sometimes difficult to avoid, is to employ terms such as 'moralistic' to describe other people's moral beliefs which we consider to be misguided.

For many years I have carried around a quotation from Bertrand Russell:

> If men were actuated by self-interest, which they are not – except in the case of a few saints – the whole human race would co-operate. There would be no more wars, no more armies, no more bombs. ...
>   I do not deny that there are better things than selfishness, and that some people achieve these things. I maintain, however, on the one hand that there are few occasions upon which large bodies of men, such as politics is concerned with, can rise above selfishness, while on the other hand, there are a great many circumstances in which populations will fall below selfishness, if selfishness is interpreted as enlightened self-interest. And among those occasions on which people fall below self-interest are most of the occasions on which they are convinced that they are acting from idealistic motives. Much that passes as idealism is disguised hatred or disguised love of power.[1]

More atrocious deeds may well have been committed through the self-righteous commitment to ill-conceived moral codes than through deliberate selfishness and greed. The Grand Inquisitor in 16th century Spain sincerely believed that the highest moral goal was the protection and advancement of the faith. When Philip II asks, in Don Carlos: '*La natura, l'amor tacer potranno in me?*' (May I not heed the voice of nature and love?), the Inquisitor replies: '*Tutto tacer dovra per esalter la fe*' (Everything must be silenced at the command of the faith).[2] If moral codes can have perverse effects when the stakes are so high, can they not also be pernicious in the normal business of economic life?

Business ethics

The subject known as business ethics is a sub-branch of economics and ethics. But it is a branch that is immensely more prosperous than the rest of the business. The subject has blossomed since the mid-1980s in the wake of a number of corporate scandals. Some 500 business ethics courses are said to be available in the USA, and the subject is taught in 90 per cent of business schools. Europe's first publication in the area was, no one should be surprised, in Italian. The spirit of the subject is captured by an *Economist* headline: 'How to be Ethical and Still Come Top'. John Kay, himself a Professor of Business Economics, has remarked:

> If Aristotle, John Stuart Mill and G.E. Moore could not sort our ethical problems once and for all, it is unlikely that today's business gurus can solve them with a few trite phrases. But, untroubled by these concerns, they go on earning more for a single lecture than Aristotle, Mill and Moore were paid in their entire lifetime.

If we want to be more charitable, we can say that business ethics is a celebration of the modern corporation – which is why corporate executives devote shareholders' funds to it. I shall come back later to discuss the supposed social responsibilities of business.

In the last resort, however, business ethics is not a real subject, as distinct from ethics generally. Some philosophers make a distinction between morality itself, which concerns how we should behave, and ethics, which they see as a more abstract analysis of the language of moral discourse. But in ordinary language ethics is used to cover both aspects, as it is here.

In this sense there is only ethics and its application to different spheres. Business, medicine, politics and law all throw up their special problems; but whatever our basic morality, it should apply to all of these fields as well as personal behaviour.

A frequent business conundrum concerns bribery. A business executive may be strongly opposed to the practice, but if he refrains from bribing some overseas government official, his competitors will obtain a lucrative order.

This dilemma is but a particular instance of the difficulty of applying the Golden Rule, 'do unto others as you would have them do unto you', when others do not observe it. In this case the practice you would like to see observed is: do not give or take bribes.

But what do you do if others will not follow? Become a martyr; or do as others actually do, even though you are endorsing a pernicious practice?

Those who are genuinely interested in moral reasoning rather than striking attitudes will not stop there. The maxim against bribery is a lower level rule of everyday morality, not a basic principle. We merely think that human welfare would be greater in a world without bribery.[3]

To say either 'never give or take bribes though the heavens fall' or 'grow up and do what others do' is an evasion. Circumstances need to be examined, including the validity of the maxim itself. In the would-be Soviet command economy the only way of matching supplies to requirements was by a series of side payments and unofficial deals between officials in state enterprises. In these circumstances, it may have been a duty to encourage such payments to help Soviet citizens lead a slightly less impoverished life. Of course, at a later stage when the command economy had broken down, the legacy of these habits did a great deal of damage. But it would hardly have been a realistic obligation to have had to guess how many decades would elapse before the collapse of the Soviet system.

How about more standard cases where we believe that the community in question would benefit from less bribery or no bribery at all? Even then we should pause before inflicting known and measurable damage on our own family's standard of living for the sake of a hypothetical gesture towards reform in a society which we may imperfectly understand.

But then reflect a little more: for the cost of observing the Golden Rule is often much less than it appears, especially in open, developed capitalist countries where the long-run returns from different kinds of enterprise tend towards equality. An example comes to mind of an Oxbridge college whose investments had plunged in a stock market slump. The head of the college glowered at his Fellows, who had insisted on a boycott of South African shares, saying that this was the kind of gesture the college could no longer afford.

In fact the cost was negligible in a highly liquid market like the stock exchange. Market prices tend to move in such a way as to equalize prospective returns on different securities, allowing for risk. So by holding the next best alternative to South African securities the college was making a negligible sacrifice.

The economics of politics
My own interest in economics and ethics comes from a different area, the subject known in the USA as 'public choice' but best understood as the 'economics of politics'. This study arose as a reaction to the pious notion that government somehow stands above the sordid self-interest of the common market-place and is subject to higher motives and purpose. This view was labelled by Harry Johnson the Fabian–Benthamite view of government. By contrast, practitioners of public choice treat politicians as operating in their own market-place, seeking votes rather than cash, in a market-place that has its own distinctive kinds of failure.

This general approach has been a salutary one, whatever one may think of the specific contents of public choice theory. But it needs to be complemented by an analysis of the positive effects of moral beliefs. Just as political actors have their normal share of self-interest, so economic actors are influenced by their views or assumptions on what is right and proper. David Hume, who has already been cited on 'ought' and 'is', penned the following observation:

Force is always on the side of the governed, the governors have nothing to support them but opinion. It is therefore on opinion that government is founded: and this maxim extends to the most despotic and the most military of governments, as well as the most free and the most popular. The soldan of Egypt, or the emperor of Rome, might drive his harmless subject, like brute beasts, against their sentiments and inclinations; but he must at least have led his mamalukes, or praetorian bands, like men, by their opinion.[4]

Hume himself does not provide too much help in developing these observations further, partly because in that particular essay he is concerned mainly with political behaviour, and even there does not attempt any systematic theory. So we have to carry on ourselves.

The debate on self-interest

While there have been many discussions of economics and ethics over the last 200 years, they have all too rarely come to grips with the effect of specific moral beliefs on behaviour. Instead we have had a ferocious but highly generalized debate on the self-interest assumption that was supposed to underly classical political economy, and the message of selfishness which market economists were supposed to preach. Or, as Carlyle put it, 'Every man for himself and the devil take the hindmost'.

Throughout most of the debate there has been a confusion between self-interest and materialism. One can imagine a world in which material desires were satisfied with the product of a very few hours work and most people spent most of their time reciting poetry and playing the harp to each other, perhaps charging for their performances. This would be a non-materialist world, but it could still be heavily influenced by self-interest. Modern economists have tried to remove this misunderstanding by saying that people try to maximize not material prospects, but an abstract quantity called utility – which is defined in a circular way to cover whatever it is that people seek or prefer.

With this amendment, many economists down to our own day have been happy to say, in George Stigler's words, that a person's utility 'depends upon the welfare of the actor, his family, plus a narrow circle of associates'. Many other thinkers, including some economists have, however, remained enraged by this assumption.

Political defenders of capitalism and competitive markets have clutched at the inclusion of family and close associates as at a straw to absolve them from the sin of preaching selfishness. But the straw cannot bear the weight.

From the genetic point of view, the pursuit of one's family's welfare is just a more extended form of selfishness. A greater concern for children, brothers or sisters than for the human race in general makes sense if survival is substituted for satisfaction as the main goal, and if the gene is substituted for the individual human-being as the maximizing agent. There is clearly much common ground between the 'selfish gene' and the self-interested economic man, and critics who dislike one usually dislike the other.

Rational problem-solving

An attempt has been made by some writers to overthrow any kind of self-interest assumption and to redefine economics as the rational problem-solving approach.[5] From this point of view people's utility depends on self-chosen objectives of any kind. These may include leading saintly lives, maximizing charitable donations or promoting their church. Moreover, their utility may depend not just on their own welfare but on that of any group, even all mankind and generations yet unborn.

The rational problem-solving approach gets rid of the spectre of pure self-seeking, but at the same time provides the foundation of 'economic imperialism' – that is, the attempt to colonize other subject areas. Radnitzky terms this approach 'universal economics', and argues that the, 'bare building blocks of the Economic Approach (EA) are optimizing and equilibrium, scarcity, opportunities, cost, preference and choice. Universal Economics is basically an invitation to straight thinking', recognizing that there are always such things as costs and benefits.

Defined in this way, economics becomes identical with what is often called decision theory. In fact this territory is no longer the monopoly of economists. Mathematicians, theoretical statisticians, biologists, cyberneticists and philosophers have all made contributions. There is, of course, nothing more trivial than the faculty building in which studies are carried out. The point is that rational decision-taking is consistent with any behaviour that is not random, motiveless and therefore demonstrably irrational. Rationality by itself is insufficient to explain the key features of economic life, for which we need both more restrictive assumptions about motivation and more information on institutions such as markets, government, property rights and so on.[6]

Successive circles

Why not move to a more realistic view of motivation, which avoids tautology, which is wider than the self-interest of the economist but narrower than the universal love of the preacher? Why not accept that most people have strong feelings of obligation towards relations and close friends, and some feelings towards colleagues, members of the same class or cultural group, race, nationality or creed. Different people would place these latter groups in different orders, so that the ordering of the successive circles of concern may vary; but the majority would have stronger feelings towards all than towards the human race in general. Why not then accept these circles as a basis for studying behaviour and assessing the performance of public authorities?

The strength of obligation towards the outer circles will vary according to the person, the time and the issue at hand. When responding to tax changes we can expect something like John Stuart Mill's economic man who 'prefers a greater proportion of wealth to a smaller'. When it comes to blood donations, people are motivated by a desire to help their fellows at modest cost. There are also high pressure periods such as war, or an old-fashioned miners' strike, when group or national loyalties override everything else. The adverse side is, of course, the intensification of hostile feelings towards outsiders: and it is fortunate that most people cannot live too long under such pressure-cooker conditions.

A test case of the strength of self-interest versus other loyalties is the so-called voting paradox – the question of why people vote when there is a vanishingly small chance that their action will influence the result. The self-interest model should have no difficulty in accommodating motives like self-expression, or the desire to be a good citizen, so long as the cost of voting is trivial – say a pleasant evening stroll to the polling booth. The self-interest model is in trouble, however, if people will go considerable distances on foot in discomfort in bad weather or in the face of attractive alternatives such as watching the 'match of the season' on television. I would expect the cost that people are prepared to bear to vote to vary a great deal: and maybe the only theories that we can generate about this will be low level and culture-based.

One amusing result, which has been frequently replicated by Robert Frank and others, is that students of economics give more narrowly self-interested answers to attitude questionnaires than other students, and tend to go for the selfish behaviour in prisoner's dilemma games. If their textbooks tell them that that is how people act for the most part, they will be afraid of looking like suckers if they act differently. They may also believe that the results of such motivation will in the end not be too bad for the others, appearances to the contrary notwithstanding.

The invisible hand
Moralists have long been upset by Adam Smith's 'invisible hand' doctrine, epitomized by the well-known quotation:

> It is not from the benevolence of the butcher, the brewer, or the baker that we expect our dinner, but from their regard of their own advantage.

Smith goes on to claim that in serving themselves they serve their fellows better than had they consciously striven to do so.

What bothers many people is the suggestion that free market economists in the tradition of Smith are urging people to be selfish. They are bemused rather than appeased by numerous other citations in which Smith emphasized the importance of sympathy with fellow men and women and, despite the work of Smith scholars, I do not think he achieved a rounded doctrine.

Extolling selfishness would, however, be a very peculiar thing for a political economist to do. Not even the most libertarian economist would urge the shooting of competitors. Nearly all economists have accepted that there are many areas where the invisible hand does not work and, even where it does, it will only work successfully against a background of laws, habits, customs and institutions – as we have already noted in the context of the former communist countries.

As I have gone into this extensively elsewhere[7], let me summarize by saying that the invisible hand makes most sense as a *prima facie* rule of conduct within a wider system of morality. My suggestion is that, in matters such as buying and selling, or in deciding what and how to produce, we would do others more good if we behave *as if* we were following our own self-interest rather than pursuing more altruistic goals. Some market-type process is necessary to yield the information that even a community of altruists would require to decide what to produce and by what methods it should be produced. Contrary to popular superstition, technology alone does not provide the answers.

The *as if* injunction must be applied with care. Even where it applies, the pursuit of self-interest must be limited by side constraints such as the observance of contracts, honesty, non-violence and so on. Moreover, there are such things as public goods which will not be provided in sufficient quantity in the market-place, because of the temptation to free ride on the efforts of others. Obvious examples are defence and the police. Moreover, there are many spheres where self-interest will only yield good results if appropriate adjustments are made to the price structure by public policy, for example the enforcement of the principle that the polluter pays.

Prisoner's dilemma
An intellectual device – invented nearly two centuries after Adam Smith – illustrating a situation where the invisible hand argument does not apply is known as the prisoner's dilemma. The danger is that anything I say on this topic will seem naive and over-simple to practitioners of game theory, while still puzzling those who are new to the topic. Let me use the simplest representation.

The dilemma runs as follows.[8] Two prisoners, held in separate cells, have been accomplices in a serious crime, for which the sentence is 20 years. The prosecutor does not have the evidence to convict either person; but he can convict both on a lesser charge involving a sentence of one year. If prisoner X confesses and incriminates Y while Y remains silent, X will go free and Y will get 20 years. If Y confesses and X does not, it will be the other way around. If both confess, each will get five years. If both stay silent, each is convicted on the lesser charge and gets one year. These various possibilities are summarized in Figure 1.1.

Prisoner Y

		Confess	Remain silent
Prisoner X	Confess	Five years each	X goes free Y gets 20 years
	Remain silent	X gets 20 years Y goes free	One year each

Figure 1.1   Co-operation and confession

If X consults only his self-interest he will confess. He examines what Y might do. Read down the columns. If Y confesses, X will get five years if he also confesses, but 20 years if he does not. If Y remains silent, X will go free if he confesses, but will get one year if he too remains silent. So, whatever Y does, X is better off confessing. Prisoner Y applies parallel reasoning. So they both confess and go to jail for five years. But if they had trusted each other and neither had confessed, they would each have received a sentence of only one year.

This story has been generalized to apply to numerous other situations – even though the prisoner's dilemma is only one of many types of game. To get away from the criminal example it is best to replace 'confess' and 'remain silent' by the less specific 'co-operate' and 'defect'.

One obvious application is that of two neighbours whose litter blows into each other's gardens unless they take precautions. The first preference of each neighbour is that the other should take precautions, allowing himself a free run. The second is that they both take precautions. The third is that neither takes precautions. The fourth and worst is that each alone should take precautions, allowing the neighbour a free run. If each reasons in isolation on the basis of self-interest, each will end with the third best outcome and a litter-strewn garden.

A different area of application is industrial training. Employer A may prefer that employer B should train workers, so that he can bid them away fully trained. Employer B may reason similarly. But if each reasons in this manner, they will end up in a situation which no one would prefer, with neither firm training workers.

A full theory of behaviour would have to divide human interactions into those where the invisible hand produces the best result, and those where a more co-operative norm works better. It might often be possible to make a two-stage division. The retail market for bread and meat will work best if certain norms of good behaviour such as 'do not sell contaminated meat' and 'do not lie about the freshness of your bread' are observed. But once these background rules are in operation, the consumer may indeed do better if the butcher and the baker follow the profit motive than if they try consciously to do something of a higher nature. They might then, for instance, try to force some food fad on us, or keep their shops open so long that their own exhaustion far outweighs any benefit to the consumer.

This ties up with the classic argument of von Mises against state planning. It is not just that workers and managers would lack the incentives to provide the right products by the right methods. Even if they were saints they would lack the information to do so.

Self-interested co-operation

So long as the game is played only once, the prisoner's dilemma remains. Each prisoner would be better off trusting the other not to confess. But unless there is fellow feeling between the two prisoners (or a gang boss threatening punishment in the background) neither will find any reason to do so.

Now assume that there is not one game, but that the game is repeated many times: then the situation is transformed. A celebrated study of repeated games of this sort was carried out in the early 1980s by an American political scientist, Robert Axelrod. He organized tournaments in which distinguished game theorists, as well as computer enthusiasts and others, played against each other on the basis of submitted computer programes. The results were surprisingly clear-cut. It pays to follow a co-operative strategy whenever your partner/opponent is co-operative, but to retaliate quickly if your partner/opponent defects. Indeed, by far the most robust strategy, which did best in a variety of environments, was the simple 'tit-for-tat' strategy that offers co-operation on the first round of the game and then reciprocates the other player's last action. Co-operate if he co-operated, defect if he defected. This strategy was submitted to Axelrod's tournaments by only one player, the distinguished game theorist and psychologist Anatol Rapaport.

Axelrod's results caused a sensation in a limited circle and, indeed, featured in a celebrated *Horizon* television programme in 1986 entitled 'Nice Guys Finish First'. These results have illuminated an astonishingly diverse range of subjects. One example is the 'live and let live' system which developed in the trench warfare of World War I, in which – to the fury of the high commands – front line soldiers refrained from shooting to kill, provided that their restraint was reciprocated.

Some of the initial enthusiasm went quite over the top. Those who had never liked economic models based on utility-maximizing individuals, or competitive markets, thought that they could have a great time burning the textbooks. But a careful reading of Axelrod's own book showed this triumphalism to be unjustified.

The players in these games are in no sense altruistic, but simply maximize long-term self-interest. As Axelrod writes: 'The foundation of co-operation is not really trust but the durability of the relationship'. Moreover, 'tit-for-tat' is far from a perfect rule. Once a feud is generated – I defect on one round and you defect on the next – it can go on indefinitely. The rule is just more effective than any other which emerged.

Writers in this area have identified several kinds of altruism. Here are a few varieties in ascending order of concern for others:

- *Kinship altruism* covers close relationships and is often explained by the demands of genetic preservation. J.B.S. Haldane once said that he should be willing to die to save eight first cousins, who between them would have the same genetic material.
- *Reciprocal altruism* is based on anticipated or actual reciprocity, as in the tit-for-tat strategies in repeated prisoner's dilemma games. Examples are frequent in the animal world, as in mutual grooming.
- *Hard core altruism* is the set of actions which are genuinely independent of personal reward or reciprocation.

The most celebrated example of hard core altruism is the Golden Rule. The well-known problem is that turning the other cheek provides an incentive for others to exploit you.

But there are also many problems with merely reciprocal altruism. It is insufficient to explain many frequently performed actions, such as returning a wallet full of money to its rightful owner, tipping in a restaurant that the diner will never visit again, or removing litter from a beach where the holiday-maker is unobserved.

The apparent success of reciprocity in repeated prisoner's dilemma games depends on there being an indefinite sequence of games. If the players know that they are in the final round of the sequence, it would pay each of them to defect in the penultimate round, knowing that each will defect in the ultimate round so that co-operation will not be reciprocated, players will also defect. Thus, it is argued, the whole sequence of games will unravel back to the non-co-operative solution. A real life temptation would be for the retiring baker to lie about the freshness of his bread, and for this to influence the trust that customers would place in bakers even before retirement.

An American economist, Robert Frank, has provided what he calls a commitment model to account for apparently selfless behaviour. The problem is that people, including the purely self-interested rationalist, would benefit from living in a world where people behave well even without the promise of reward or the threat of punishment.

This problem could be overcome if enough people could make a firm commitment which would govern their actions in most foreseeable circumstances. In everyday life the best sign of such a commitment is a reputation – for instance, for honest behaviour even when it might pay to cheat. Such a reputation has its rewards. Other people are willing to enter into transactions with such a reputable person without incurring the costs of intense scrutiny.

It might seem that the best of all worlds for the self-interested person is to acquire a reputation for honesty, without actually being honest, so that he could cheat when he could get away with it. Frank's principal point is that such deception is not as easy as it looks. The best way to appear honest is to be honest, and dissembling carries tell-tale signs. He interprets this in behaviourist terms as 'feeling bad' or blushing when indulging in unworthy conduct.

Frank argues that insincere professors of co-operative or trustworthy behaviour often give themselves away, and he cites a great deal of psychological evidence. Thus people will actually satisfy their selfish interests best if they commit themselves to behaving altruistically – just as the best way to achieve happiness or spontaneity is not to strive too obviously in these directions.

Stated in this way, altruism looks like long-term enlightened self-interest of the 'honesty is the best policy' kind. Indeed there is something paradoxical about sincere concern for others as a route to a person's own well-being. Is this genuine morality, or is it higher level prudence? Moreover, how can the two be distinguished?

In Frank's own account there is a niche for those pretending to have a good-citizen disposition without actually having it. For although insincerity tends to be detected, there are costs to detection. If the overwhelming majority of the population is honest, it might not be worth incurring the costs of guarding against the occasional dishonest person, and this allows a niche for some dishonest people. In one of his key hypothetical examples, Frank finds that the maximum gain from co-operation is achieved when 75 per cent of the population are committed co-operators and 25 per cent are opportunistic defectors. Very illuminating, but hardly the Sermon on the Mount, or the categorical imperative. In the end Frank admits that, 'the commitment model is less a disavowal of self-interest than a friendly amendment. Without abandoning the materialist framework, it suggests how the noble strand of human nature might have emerged and prospered'.[9]

Recent attempts to improve on the tit-for-tat strategy demonstrate even more clearly how far the suggested rules of this type are from genuine altruistic feeling for fellow human beings.

One weakness of tit-for-tat, already mentioned, is the danger of getting into a counter-productive feud. Suppose that, for some reason, player Y has defected in a previous round; then X defects in the current round and is emulated by Y, and so on to the end of time. Another weakness is that no advantage is taken of a 'sucker' who is willing to co-operate even when his partner does not.

A variant strategy, known as 'Pavlov', has been devised by Nowak and others to overcome these weaknesses.[10] If the tournament has degenerated into a feud, Pavlov will initiate a co-operative move and, if Y reciprocates, Pavlov will continue to co-operate. In simple terms, Pavlov will make occasional speculative forays in search of co-operation. If, however, the game has settled down into a stable pattern of co-operation, Pavlov will try an occasional defection (selected by randomizing). If Y turns out to be a 'sucker' and continues to co-operate, Pavlov will repeat the defection; otherwise it will return to co-operation. Thus there will be both more appeasement and more aggression under Pavlov than under straightforward tit-for-tat. But in all cases the self-interested motivation stands out clearly.

Effects of specific rules

I suggest that the argument about self-interested versus co-operative man has reached the point of rapidly diminishing returns. What we need is an examination of specific co-operative rules to see whether they in fact improve on the results of self-interest or whether they make matters worse.[11]

This last possibility is suggested by the original setting of the prisoner's dilemma. If both prisoners follow a co-operative strategy and remain silent, two criminals escape punishment for a serious crime. Co-operation is only beneficial from the point of view of the criminals – thus illustrating the logic of 'honour among thieves'. But from the point of view of the rest of us, it is much better that one or both prisoners should confess.

Which of the constraints on narrow self-interest are of the perverse kind – as when the two criminals escape with reduced sentences – and which are of the benign kind – as when each householder sweeps the snow from in front of their own house in the expectation that others will do the same? As there has been little systematic study, I can only enumerate a few examples.

Let me start with one case, where the drift of the analysis so far is on the side of the co-operative norm being benign. This is the well-known argument of the late Richard Titmuss that voluntary blood donation is more efficient than commercial systems, because voluntary donors have no incentive to lie about the quality of their blood. If sufficient blood is forthcoming on a voluntary basis, all well and good. But if not, some way has to be found of monitoring commercial supplies, despite the difficulties.

A clear-cut example of harmful co-operation is the operation of a collusive cartel. Here each member refrains from selling below an agreed minimum price. The successful operation of a cartel is likely to be against the public interest, first because consumers have to pay a higher price for the product, and secondly because too little of that product will be produced and resources will be allocated inefficiently. The last is a more subtle point which will occur mainly to economists; but it is the more fundamental because it remains true even if the members of the cartel are poorer than the rest of us or specially deserving of increased income.

A further example of a pernicious 'moral' influence – one given by Frank – concerns US operators of ski lifts. Operators' investments in both acreage and equipment are chosen with weekend peak demand in mind. Weekend visitors are thus responsible for nearly all the costs associated with the ski facilities. Moreover, a heavy differential charge at weekends would reduce queues and entice more off-peak skiers onto the slopes. Yet in practice price differentials are much too small either to reflect cost differences or to avoid long queues at peak times. Operators apparently fear alienating the public's sense of fairness. Similar considerations explain why price differentials at barbers' shops on Saturday morning, or popular restaurants on weekend evenings are, when they exist at all, far too small.

Thus, the public's sense of fairness may be based on a misapprehension about facts and causes. Skiers focus on the operating costs of lifts, which are much the same at all times, without asking what determines capacity. Barbers' customers focus on the cost of the barber's time without worrying about investment in extra chairs or saloon capacity, let alone the dissatisfaction of waiting a long time for a haircut.

It might be a mistake to rush into a crusade for higher peak prices without further reflection. Both biological behaviour and evolved social institutions may serve purposes which are not immediately obvious. Traditional rules, as Hayek warns us, often contain more embodied wisdom than any individual critic can hope to have. Such respect for existing institutions can, however, provide no more than an amber light for caution. It is doubtful, for instance, whether excessively low price differentials at ski resorts have any such deeper social function.

'Vengeance is mine'

There is indeed more than one way in which a seemingly good-neighbour strategy can do harm. It can be against the interests of the rest of the community – as in the prisoner's dilemma and cartel examples – or it can be counter-productive even from the point of view of the participating individuals themselves. This latter possibility arises when a strategy is selected that appears to be co-operative, but is inappropriate at a deeper level. Most real-world situations are more complicated than the simple prisoner's dilemma, and the possibility of choosing an inappropriate strategy is a real one.

This possibility arises because the way in which strategies are normally determined is via the application of widely accepted rules – whether these are obviously moral, such as 'do not kill'; conventional, such as 'drive on the left'; or habitual such as 'do not scatter litter'.

But many widely supported moral practices and rules are distinctly double-edged. Frank cites a hypothetical Jones who sacrifices a day's earnings of $300 to prosecute Smith for stealing a $200 briefcase. The motive here can only be described as vengeance. Frank is inclined to regard Jones as a social benefactor because his action discourages theft.

Maybe. But encouraging vengeance as a general practice is playing with fire. It is vengeance for real or imagined past wrongs that is stirring up the conflict in the former Yugoslavia, Northern Ireland and between Israel and the Arabs. 'Vengeance is mine; I will repay saith the Lord'.[12]

Social responsibility of business

In which category should one put such movements as *Business in the Community*? According to one of its documents (Grayson, 1992) it stands for 'companies using some of their people, their expertise, their surplus product, premises and equipment, and sometimes cash to help tackle problems like urban deprivation, school–business links, job creation and environmental improvements'.

There is a systematic ambiguity here, as in nearly all the talk about socially responsible business. Do the proponents claim that these extra activities will indeed help a business's long-term profitability? Or do they assert that a business should follow different objectives?

For, as Elaine Sternberg (1992) points out: 'If, for example, a corporation looks like a business and portrays itself as a business, then it encourages the reasonable expectation that maximising long-term owners' value is its objective and guiding principle'. A corporation which makes its decisions on 'some other undisclosed criterion is a particularly dangerous sort of loose cannon, whether that other end is imperial, ideological or just personal'.

Grayson (1992) is full of *bien pensant* clichés, such as a shift away from 'me-ism' toward 'us-ism', 'value-driven companies' (all rational conduct is value-driven), 'making employees feel part of a team', 'public–private part-nership', 'empowerment', 'holistic approach' and, of course, 'caring'. But the basic ambiguity remains. The author insists that the movement has 'a strong business rationale', but also warns against 'activities claimed to be helping the community which are really for the company's benefit'.

Socially responsible businessmen (and their slogan-writers) regard any ques-tioning of their rationale as an attack on objectives such as urban renewal, support for the arts or employee welfare facilities. And if one is not careful they will insinuate that one is to the right of Genghis Khan, not to speak of being a monetarist.

The point that the critics should be making, however, is that the corporate responsibility movement lacks the legitimacy of either the market or the political process. It is up to the individual citizen to decide how much to devote to such causes, whether individually or collectively via elected representatives. It is not for managers to set themselves up as taxing authorities over funds which belong to shareholders – who may be their own employees or other workers investing through their pension funds.

Moreover, people function best if they have specific responsibilities. If a businessman is partly responsible for government policy, and a government official sees himself as partly responsible for the profitability of companies, then everyone becomes responsible for everything in general, and no one is responsible for anything in particular.

There is a further objection to the fashionable cult of the businessman as the person to run, and advise on, everything. For I often wonder how the favoured executives have time to manage their own companies if they are also supposed to sit on hospital boards, run quangos and have a chance of normal family life and leisure. I suspect that the business leadership which both the Thatcher and the Major Governments have tried to introduce in many semi-governmental areas is a facade behind which the old-time professionals just carry on as before.

The constitutional liberal is not arguing that the pursuit of market objectives is enough. He is saying that if there are market failures or inadequacies, it is up to the government to set up incentives for different behaviour by taxes or subsidies, or if necessary by regulation or financing of public services. Income can be redistributed via the tax and social security system. The government can intervene to improve incentives for training or for letting homes. But it is not for corporations to take on a pseudo-governmental role.

I have deliberately exaggerated. For the weakness of what I have called the constitutionalist position is that it falls into the trap I have earlier castigated of supposing that government will conform to some textbook model. But of course official programmes will be driven or distorted by interest groups, or by the providers of public services. Education, training and environmental programmes will often be very different from those which would do much to help.

As corporate executives may have dispersed local knowledge, why not make use of them? All right; so long as we recognize the limitations. Even our imperfectly enfranchised shareholders will ensure that companies do not devote more than a small proportion of their resources to non-bottom-line activities. So, both the business enthusiast and the government are deceiving themselves if they expect socially responsible businesses to carry the public policy load. My final reservation about business responsibility is that it is an attempt to achieve public policy objectives on the cheap and on the side.

Codes that kill jobs

The area where popular morality clashes most with market principles is in the labour market.

There is evidence that firms with higher profits pay higher wages to employees of any given skill level. This may appear to be common sense, but anyone who has taken a course in market economics will ask why workers do not drift from low wage firms and bid for jobs in high wage firms until pay is roughly equalized.

Some labour economists believe that they can explain the persistence of inter-firm wage differentials by a theory called 'efficiency wages'. In this theory a profitable firm will pay above market-clearing wages to motivate employees and obtain better performance. Profitable firms will also see higher rates of pay as a rationing device to enable them to pick and choose among potential workers with equal paper qualifications. The validity of efficiency wage theory is a topic of its own. While it may help to explain why pay does not move quickly to market-clearing levels, it is less successful in explaining long-lasting differentials. I would agree with Frank that part of the explanation lies in the prevalence of 'moral' beliefs that profitable firms should share some of their surplus with workers and – equally importantly – the widespread toleration for less profitable firms who can only afford to pay lower rates.

But I am less than sure that the outcome is a good one. The net effect is to retard the movement of resources from less to more efficient firms and thus hold down national income, without any clear distributional benefit.

Controversy becomes much fiercer when we come to a different set of practices: the minimum pay levels enforced by legislation or collective agreements – or other kinds of cost imposed on employers by measures of a 'European social charter' kind. Such policies are supported by the popular belief that it is wrong to encourage anything that smacks of undercutting by workers bidding for a job, or by employers trying to obtain workers on the cheap.

How reasonable is this anti-undercutting mentality? The one near certainty to hold on to in the heat of debate is that, if the loosening of minimum pay laws or their equivalents increases total employment, then the income of the whole community will be higher.

There are likely to be low income losers. Some of the workers priced into jobs may be worse off than they were on social security, taking travel costs and other add-ons into account. Even if all newly taken-on workers are no worse off, their entry is likely to worsen the pay of the less well paid already in work.

Thus, a reasonable condition for eliminating minimum wages is that those priced into work should not receive less than they received on social security.

This can be done with the aid of a top-up like the present UK Family Benefit, provided it can be extended to families without children and single people, and the conditions for claiming are made less restrictive.

The more difficult people to compensate are those already in work earning above, but not too much above, the social security minimum, whose wages will fall in the new equilibrium. Complete compensation for the distributional effects of all market changes is hardly compatible with a dynamic economy. Nevertheless, some softening of the blow would be desirable. A basic or minimum guaranteed income, with a high cut-off rate, or marginal tax rate, is the most likely bet. This could be achieved by adjusting existing social security payments and need not involve a vast new scheme. The more selective social security becomes, the more generous governments can be with top-up payments.

There is a still more difficult hornets' nest, which I can only stir and not really tackle. This is the high unemployment in OECD countries, and particularly in Europe, that prevails over the business cycle and even in boom periods. For it is now possible that quite a big fall in average real pay would be required to price into work enough people to satisfy even a modest definition of full employment.

Let me score an own goal here by stressing that national estimates of the responsiveness of employment to real pay changes may be over-optimistic (a typical example is that if pay costs were 1 per cent less, employment would be 0.5 to 1 per cent higher). For a large part of the hypothetical employment growth from lower real labour costs arises from gains in market share at the expense of other countries. The relevant question is: what would have to happen to real remuneration in the OECD area as a whole if, say, one half of those presently unemployed are to be priced back into work?

Extreme neoclassical economists dodge some of the deeper questions of moral attitudes and social practices by assuming that all unemployment is ultimately voluntary, and determined mechanistically by the social security floor. They therefore avoid having to debate popular attitudes head-on. And if they cannot get away with arguing for a lower dole, they try to argue for a less attractive dole by making the conditions for drawing the dole more stringent or forcing people who draw it to undertake some kind of training or token performance (workfare).

They therefore leave it to the less mechanistic market economists to face the popular fire by arguing with attitudes which hold pay rates well above market-clearing rates in segments of the labour market well above the social security floor.

Pay rates, employment regulations and other employment add-ons have now discouraged employers from taking on workers for so long that investment has had a labour-saving bias. A shift towards more market-related pay rates and differentials, sufficient to price people back into jobs, even gradually, would still increase national income. But it is possible that more than 100 per cent of the increase would accrue to owners of capital and land. Some extra tax on capital or income from capital could surely be justified to cushion the shock, although not so much as to kill the labour-using investment required.

I make the suggestion, not as a cure-all, but to indicate the impasse which we have reached as a result of the collision between popular attitudes towards just rewards and the requirements of high employment.

Conclusions

The market is only one part of a well-functioning economic system; and many surrounding policies, practices and habits of mind are required to obtain good value from the market system. Yet a functioning market core is still indispensable.

Matthew Parris, in one of his excellent tongue-in-cheek newspaper columns, has reminded us that most people do not accept the market system – not even to the extent that a Labour Chancellor, Social Democrat Finance Minister or Democrat US Secretary of the Treasury would want them to.

Parris writes of an aunt of his who believes that there is such a thing as a fair price or wage that can be determined by contemplation rather than the state of the market. 'To my aunt – who votes Conservative, takes the *Daily Telegraph* and regards socialism as the work of the devil – a fair price is what will secure a reasonable profit after paying employees a decent wage.' Presumably her idea of a decent wage is her impression of the average of the last few decades corrected for inflation.

I have made a few soundings of my own among business journalists, who might be expected to have a higher degree of sophistication. But even here I find great resistance to the allocational and market-clearing functions of pay and prices.

It is not that such people are rabid egalitarians. Parris's aunt is not, and I doubt if my professional colleagues are either. They can nearly all understand the incentive role of pay and prices. They also accept – if anything too readily – the hierarchies and financial differentials of modern life. And they all operate against a background in which 'prices' means the general level of prices, which they would like to see as stable as possible.

What still meets with blank incomprehension – even among people who can perform textbook exercises – is the role of relative prices, including pay. The elementary point, demonstrated by von Mises, of the role of relative prices in allocating resources and reducing queues, even in a community bathed in mutual love, has little meaning even for the educated public.

As Parris says, 'our morality does not mesh with our economic system; but because we need both they cohabit in an awkward marriage based on silence'. A dialogue – suspended since the time that Dickens, Ruskin and Shaw thundered at 19th century political economists – will have to resume. I am not suggesting that Parris's aunt should begin a course in either moral philosophy or economics. What is needed is more critical scrutiny, both of widely accepted moral beliefs and their role in economic activity, and of the moral implications of widely advocated economic policies. The idea of technocratic value-free economics has had its day.

Notes

1. Russell (1992) pp. 173–4, first published in 1954.
2. Interestingly enough this is clearer in the Verdi opera from which I have quoted than in the original Schiller play.
3. Anyone who finds this surprising or who wants to pursue the matter further should look at my *Two Cheers for Utilitarianism*, which appears as chapter two of Brittan (1983).
4. Hume (1985) pp. 32–3.
5. A guide to this approach is available in Radnitzky (1993).
6. A tour of some of the complexities and philosophical issues raised by modern decision theory can be found in Nozick (1992). But I fear that his fraternization with 'symbolic utility' can only give comfort to practitioners of 'political correctness'.
7. Brittan (1988) especially pp. 12–13 and 230–34.
8. The prisoner's dilemma is supposed to have been invented around 1950 by Merrill Flood and Melvin Dresler, and stated formally soon after by the mathematician A.W. Tucker.
9. Commitment problems also come up in a very different branch of economics – namely counter-inflationary policy. How do you prevent government from giving the economy an inflationary boost before elections, when the immediate effects are often pleasant with the inflationary costs delayed until well after polling day? There is a genuine advantage in having monetary authorities with a good reputation for avoiding such behaviour.

    An ultra-rationalist might believe that electorates will see through such tactics and that prudent policies will be adopted by governments out of self-interest. Others find it helpful to have a commitment device by which the government binds its hands in advance. The two favourite devices are an independent central bank and an exchange rate link to a country with sound money credibility, as Germany had until recently

    An independent central bank is for the moment more fashionable than the currency link. But all these devices – including a trustworthy reputation – may break down if the pressure on them is large enough. So, I imagine, would the commitment of Frank's honest man – for instance, if he were to find a sufficiently large wallet in a sufficiently lonely place, and could appease his conscience by donating a proportion of the gain to charity. So the greater credibility of an independent central bank over a government is a matter of degree.
10. See Nowak and Sigmund (1993) and Beardsley (1993) for further discussion.
11. These co-operative rules belong to what John Stuart Mill called the 'intermediate generalizations' of popular morality, which are subordinate to higher order ethical principles, in his case the principle of utility. The contemporary moral philosopher, Richard Hare, makes a similar distinction between intuitive and critical levels.
12. St Paul, Epistle to the Romans.

Bibliography

Axelrod, R. (1990), *The Evolution of Co-operation*, Harmondsworth: Penguin Books.
Beardsley, T. (1993), 'Never Give a Sucker an Even Break', *Scientific American*, October.
Brittan, S. (1983), 'Two Cheers for Utilitarianism', in *The Role and Limits of Government*, London: Temple Smith.
Brittan, S. (1988), *A Restatement of Economic Liberalism*, London: Macmillan.
Dunkley, C. (1993), 'Ethos of Vans, Doors and Bosnia', in *Financial Times*, 4 August.
The Economist (1993), 'How to be Ethical and Still Come Top', in *The Economist*, 5 June.
Frank, R. (1988), *Passions Within Reason*, New York and London: W.W. Norton.

Grayson, D. (1992), *Corporate Community Involvement as a Strategic Managerial Tool*, Durham: Durham University Business School.

Hausman, D.M. and McPherson, M.S. (1993), 'Taking Ethics Seriously: Economics and Contemporary Moral Philosophy', *Journal of Economic Literature*, **XXXI** (2), 671–731.

Hume, D. (1777), 'Of the First Principles of Government', in Miller, E. (ed.), *Essays Moral Political and Literary*, Indianapolis: Liberty Classics (1985).

Kay, J. (1993) 'How the Ethics Men Miss the Point', in *Daily Telegraph*, 5 July.

Nowak, M. and Sigmund, K. (1993), 'A Strategy of Win–Stay Lose–Shift', *Nature*, **364**, July 1.

Nozick, R. (1992), *The Nature of Rationality*, Princeton: Princeton University Press.

Parris, M. (1992), 'It is Unhealthy…', in *The Times*, 21 December.

Radnitzky, G. (ed.) (1993), *Universal Economics*, New York: Paragon House.

Russell, B. (1992), *Human Society in Ethics and Politics*, London: Routledge.

Sen, A.K. (1970), *Collective Choice and Social Welfare*, San Fransisco: Holden Day.

Smith, A. (1776), *An Inquiry into the Nature and Causes of the Wealth of Nations*, Indianapolis: Liberty Classics (1981).

Smith, A. (1759), *The Theory of Moral Sentiments*, Indianapolis: Liberty Classics (1982).

Sternberg, E. (1992), 'The Responsible Shareholder', *Business Ethics*, July.

Stigler, G. (1981), *The Tanner Lectures on Human Values*, Cambridge: Cambridge University Press.

2   Moral codes and economic success
Amartya Sen[1]

Introduction

Do moral codes of behaviour have anything to offer in achieving economic
success? The answer that much of modern economics seems to take for granted
is definitely 'no'. Good performance in business is supposed to depend on hard-
nosed cultivation of self-interest. Indeed, the so-called 'economic method' that
many economists have attempted to impose not just on economics, but also on
other social disciplines, asks that analysts see behaviour in terms of preference
fulfilment and the intelligent pursuit of self-interest, steering clear of the deontic
demands of morals and values. This is taken to be the best explanation of
behaviour and also a fine basis for achieving whatever good results the market
mechanism has to offer. To do one's moral duty may be good for one's soul,
but it is not, so the argument goes, particularly wonderful for business or for
the economy.

Perhaps the most widely quoted aphorism in economics is Adam Smith's
remark about the butcher, the brewer and the baker in *The Wealth of Nations*
(a remark that is cited with such exclusiveness by many economists that one is
inclined to wonder whether anything else of Smith is any longer read):

> It is not from the benevolence of the butcher, the brewer, or the baker that we expect
> our dinner, but from their regard to their own interest. We address ourselves, not to
> their humanity but to their self-love. ... [2]

The butcher, the brewer and the baker want to earn money from us, and we –
the consumers – want the meat, the beer and the bread they have to sell. The
exchange benefits us all. There would seem to be no need for any moral codes
in bringing about the betterment of all the parties involved. What is needed is
simply some 'self-love' on our parts, and the market can apparently be relied
upon to do the rest in bringing about the mutually gainful exchanges.

In this chapter I shall try to examine the nature and limits of this claim. It is
a matter of some practical interest in assessing the determinants of economic
performance in different parts of the world – varying from economic development in the Third World and economic reform in what used to be called the
Second World, to the variable performance of different economies in the First
World. I shall end by taking the opportunity to discuss some of the specific issues
that have been thrown up by the recent Italian debates on the need to tackle
corruption – and even the influence of the Mafia.[3]

Adam Smith on motives and behaviour

There is a well-known oddity in seeing Adam Smith as the great champion of 'self-love', and in viewing that tireless Professor of Moral Philosophy as the no-nonsense scoffer at the importance of moral codes. As a matter of fact, Smith spent much of his life arguing for the need for 'sympathy' in other-regarding conduct and exploring the role of 'moral sentiments' in making the world a better place. This is not the occasion to carry out a detailed discussion of Adam Smith's views and recommendations, but I shall begin with a few clarifying comments on what Smith was saying – and in particular what he was *not* saying.[4] Some of the distinctions invoked are, I believe, of some general interest – going well beyond the part they play in explaining Smith's beliefs.

In fact, in his *The Theory of Moral Sentiments*, Smith went extensively into the role of moral codes of behaviour. He also distinguished between distinct reasons for going against the dictates of self-love, including *inter alia* the following:

- *sympathy* 'the most humane actions require no self-denial, no self-command, no great exertion of the sense of priority', and 'consist only in doing what this exquisite sympathy would of its own accord prompt us to do';
- *generosity* 'it is otherwise with generosity', when 'we sacrifice some great and important interest of our own to an equal interest of a friend or of a superior';
- *public spirit* 'when he compares those two objects with one another, he does not view them in the light in which they naturally appear to himself, but in that in which they appear to the nation he fights for'.[5]

In some of these choices the person's basic 'sympathy' does the work spontaneously, while in others he has to make the 'impartial spectator enter into the principles of his conduct'.[6]

Smith's admiration of Stoic philosophy was much at peace with the views about correct conduct that he came to propound. He discussed extensively the need for non-self-interested behaviour. While 'prudence was of all virtues that which is most helpful to the individual', Smith argued that 'humanity, justice, generosity, and public spirit, are the qualities most useful to others'.[7] Through overlooking Smith's wide-ranging writings, and by concentrating on only a few selected passages (such as the one on the baker–brewer–butcher deal), the father of modern economics has too often been made to look like a narrow-minded ideologue – incessantly outlining the pristine virtues of selfish behaviour. While some men are born small and some achieve smallness, Adam Smith has had much smallness thrust upon him.[8]

Exchange, production and motivation

The point is sometimes made that even though Smith acknowledged the fruitful role of moral codes of behaviour in social and political matters, his views of useful motivations in economics were fairly well reflected by the butcher–brewer–baker remark. The resolution of the so-called 'Adam Smith problem' through this division of fields has appealed to many economists.

But what was Smith really saying in this passage? Clearly, Smith was arguing here that the pursuit of self-interest would be fine to motivate the exchange of commodities, and we do not need to invoke much morality in explaining why the baker wants to sell bread and we want to buy it, and how that exchange benefits us both. As an observation full of homely wisdom this is a fine enough remark, but admirers of Smith – and this writer is second to none in this respect – must be grateful that he wrote much else.

One question we have to ask to measure the claim of the butcher–brewer–baker aphorism is this: *Do economic operations and activities consist only of exchanges of this kind?* What about such economic activities as production, requiring team spirit and collaborative work on the factory floor? Did Smith think that production was an unimportant part of economics?

Secondly, we have also to ask the question: *Is the basic motivation of desiring exchange all that is needed to have successful exchanges?*

Would Smith have thought that the result of the pursuit of exchange would be just as good if the businesses involved, driven by self-interest, were to try to defraud the consumers? What about trusting each other's words and having confidence in the reliability of the offers and promises that others make?

The answers to these questions are not hard to find. First, economic operations encompass many activities other than exchange, notably production, and the motivational problems underlying production can be very different from those in exchange. They involve the difficult task of generating effective co-operation in the work-place despite considerable conflict of interest (combined with partial congruence). The importance of dutiful activity, unsupervised reliability and a concern for efficiency can hardly be overstated in discussing the determinants of economic productivity. Whether we attempt to understand the deep production problems in the reforming experience of the former Soviet Union and Eastern Europe, or try to explain the Japanese economic success *vis-à-vis* British or American difficulties, we cannot get very much insight from the alleged fecundity of our butcher–brewer–baker's desire to exchange.

Secondly, even within the field of exchange (ignoring production for the moment), its efficiency can be much influenced by trust between the different parties. If self-interest were the only concern (and the only determinant of behaviour), there would be many occasions on which letting the other side down (for example by reneging on earlier arrangements) would be sensible enough. To rely just on legal recourse would make business activities expensive and slow.

Something more than noticing that there is gain from trade is involved in making exchange an efficient activity. The sense of trust and the use of behavioural codes in this context may well be analysed in primarily ethical terms – invoking, say, Kant's principles of 'universalizability', or Smith's own 'impartial spectator'. Alternatively, it is possible to bring in some game-theoretic reasoning to explain the emergence and survival of moral codes. But no matter which route we take, the need for such codes of behaviour for efficient transactions would be hard to overlook. The business world shorn of moral codes is not only normatively indigent, it can also be very poor in performance.[9]

Institutions, trust and economic activities

The trouble with reading much into the homely butcher–brewer–baker example is not only that it ignores the role of moral codes in (1) non-exchange activities (such as production), and (2) in non-motivational aspects of exchange activities themselves (such as the need for mutual reliability), but also that it downplays the function of *institutions* that sustain and promote economic activities. The concern of the different parties with their own interests certainly can *motivate* people to take part in exchange from which each benefits. But whether the exchange will operate well will depend also on organizational conditions. There is a need for institutional development which can take quite some time to emerge – a lesson that is currently being learned rather painfully in Eastern Europe and the former Soviet Union. The importance of institutions was rather eclipsed there in the first flush of enthusiasm about the magic of allegedly automatic market processes.

The need for institutional development has some clear connection with the role of codes of behaviour, since institutions based on interpersonal arrangements and shared understandings operate on the basis of common behaviour patterns, mutual trust and confidence in the behavioural ethics of each other. The reliance on rules of behaviour may typically be implicit rather than explicit – indeed so implicit that its importance can be easily overlooked in situations in which such confidence is unproblematic. But whenever it is *not* unproblematic, the overlooking of its need can be quite disastrous. This is a particularly important issue in many specific contexts, such as: (1) economic development (in the Third World), (2) economic reform (in the former Second World), and (3) relative productivity and avoidance of corruption (even in the First World).

But it would be a mistake to see moral codes in all-or-nothing terms. The nature of the codes does vary and so does their effectiveness in promoting economic success. While capitalism has been very successful in radically enhancing output and raising productivity in the modern world, it is still the case that the experiences of different countries are quite diverse. The recent experiences of East Asian economies – most notably Japan – raise important questions about the modelling of capitalism in traditional economic theory. To see capitalism as a system of pure profit-maximization based on individual ownership of capital is to leave out much that has made the system such a success in raising output and in generating income.

I am personally no great admirer of unrestrained capitalism. I think it is no tribute to the system that African Americans (that is, American blacks) have lower chances of survival to an advanced age than do the citizens of China or the Indian state of Kerala (despite their poverty but with reasonable systems of public health care).[10] It is also striking that men in the Harlem region of the prosperous city of New York have lower survival chances than their corresponding number in even famished Bangladesh. The lack of health care and other public services even with high average income can be terribly debilitating for society. Also, the omnipresence of aggression and fear in modern urban life in great centres of capitalism is nothing short of revolting. Capitalism has been distinctly less successful in shaping the political economy of a just society than in dramatically raising the average level of opulence.

But I would still argue that as far as the *successes* of capitalism are concerned (such as opening up the possibility of standards of living that people could not have dreamt of even a few generations ago), to see them all as the unintended result of pure greed is to belittle the system altogether. Capitalism has made it possible to raise productivity by team-work, by co-ordination and co-operation, and ultimately by trust in each other's behaviour in economic and business relationships. Codes of behaviour have been central to this achievement. While some have criticized this pervasive co-operation given the unequal outcomes (Marx's treatment of 'false consciousness' of the working class related to the ideological neglect of this contrast), and others have seen in it one of the untarnished glories of modern industrial capitalism (the glowing rhetoric of President Reagan's populist economics derived much from it), it is impossible to overlook the far-reaching role of this phenomenon in generating the successes that capitalism has achieved.

On taking Japan seriously
Japan is often seen as the greatest example of successful capitalism. However, the motivation pattern that dominates Japanese business has much more content than would be provided by pure profit-maximization. Different commentators have emphasized distinct aspects of Japanese motivational features. Michio Morishima (1982) has outlined the special characteristics of the 'Japanese ethos' as emerging from its particular history of rule-based behaviour patterns. Ronald Dore has seen the influence of 'Confucian ethics'.[11] Masahiko Aoki (1989) has seen co-operation and behavioural codes in terms that are more responsive to game-theoretic reasoning. There are other behaviour-based accounts related to Japanese economic performance.[12]

There is, in fact, some truth even in the apparently puzzling claim made in *The Wall Street Journal* that Japan is 'the only communist nation that works'.[13] It points to the non-profit motivations underlying many economic and business activities in Japan. We have to understand and interpret the peculiar fact that what is arguably the most successful capitalist nation in the world flourishes economically with a motivation structure that departs firmly from the pursuit of self-interest, which – we have been told – is the bedrock of capitalism.

Japan does not, by any means, provide the only example of a powerful role of business ethics in promoting capitalist success. The merits of selfless work and devotion to enterprise in raising productivity have been seen as important for economic achievements in many countries in the world. Indeed, capitalism's need for motivational structures more complex than pure profit-maximization has been acknowledged in various forms, over a long time, by many leading social scientists (though not by many 'mainstream' economists). One thinks of Marx, Weber, Tawney and others.[14] The role of non-profit motives in the success of capitalism is not a new point, even though the wealth of historical evidence and conceptual arguments in that direction is often thoroughly ignored in contemporary professional economics.

Public goods and the motivational challenge

In order to understand how motives other than self-seeking can have an important role, we have to see the limited reach of the butcher–brewer–baker argument in dealing with what modern economists call 'public goods', where one person's consumption does not exclude that of another. Whereas, say, a toothbrush is a 'private' good (your brush is for your use only), an uncrowded park or 'common' is a 'public' good (your use of it does not preclude mine).

In the case of public goods, the rationale of the self-interest-based market mechanism comes under severe strain. The market system works by putting a price on a commodity, and the allocation between consumers is done by the respective willingness to buy it at the prevailing price. When 'equilibrium prices' emerge, they balance demand with supply for each commodity. In contrast, in the case of public goods, the uses are – largely or entirely – non-competitive, and the system of giving a good to the highest bidder does not have much merit, since one person's consumption does not exclude that of another. Instead, optimum resource allocation would require that the *combined* benefits be compared with the costs of production, and here the market mechanism, based on profit-maximization, functions badly.[15]

There are two important issues to be addressed in this context, in analysing the organization and performance of production. First, there would tend to be some failure in resource allocation when the commodities produced are public goods or involve strong externalities. This can be taken *either* (1) as an argument for having publicly owned enterprises, which would be governed by principles other than profit-maximization, *or* (2) as a case for public regulations governing private enterprise, *or* (3) as establishing a need for the use of non-profit values – particularly of social concern – in private decisions (perhaps because of the goodwill that it might generate). Since public enterprises have not exactly covered themselves with glory in recent years, and public regulations – while often useful – are sometimes quite hard to implement, the third option has become more important in public discussions. It is difficult, in this context, to escape the argument for encouraging business ethics, going well beyond the traditional values of honesty and reliability, and taking on social responsibility as well (for example, in matters of environmental degradation and pollution).

The second issue is more complex and less recognized in the literature, but is also more interesting. Even in the production of private commodities there can be an important 'public good' aspect in the production process itself. This is because production is a joint activity, supervisions are costly and often unfeasible, and each participant contributes to the shared success of the firm in a way that cannot be fully reflected in the private rewards that he or she gets.

The overall success of the firm is, to a great extent, a public good, from which there is common benefit, to which all contribute, and which is not divided up into little parcels of person-specific rewards, strictly linked with each person's respective contribution. And this is precisely where motives other than narrow self-seeking become critical for productivity.

Corruption, crime and behavioural codes

The issues of collaborative efforts and productivity are not the only ones that make it important to consider the role of moral codes of behaviour in economic performance in advanced capitalist countries. Problems related to behavioural codes that have received most attention in recent deliberations involve economic corruption and its linkages with organized crime. In Italian discussions on this subject, the role of 'deontological codes' has been much invoked. The possible use of such codes in combating illegal and unfair procedures in influencing public policy has received attention, and this line of remedy has been considered even as a way of reducing the hold of the Mafia on government operations.[16]

There are two issues of behavioural codes that closely relate to this question. First, can behavioural norms be changed in the direction of some deontological codes, making a direct impact on the situation? Secondly, is the powerful influence of the Mafia indirectly related to some behavioural features influencing the operation of economic transactions?

Taking up the former question first, certainly a code of honour and a sense of duty on the part of businessmen and politicians can make a real difference to corruption, illegal transaction and the related developments of organized crime. It is not surprising that a call for such a deontological 'codice' has come from many quarters – intellectuals, businessmen, political leaders. The real questions to consider are: Can it actually work? How will it operate and with what effects?

This is, of course, an ancient issue. In *The Laws*, Plato had discussed the benefits of a strong sense of duty on the part of public servants, but had also noted that to develop that sense of duty is 'no easy task'. In the *Arthasastra*, Kautilya, the Indian political analyst of the fourth century BC, expressed great scepticism about the possibility of preventing corruption through deontology, and opted for a system of stochastically organized spot-checks followed by penalties and rewards (much as modern economics would suggest). Many of the contemporary commentators in Italy are no less sceptical of the possibility of making any significant change in behavioural modes – changes that could make a real difference in fighting corruption and organized crime. It is not hard to understand that scepticism. Reform of behaviour modes is hard to bring about through a policy decision. 'Thou should behave better' sounds like a hopeless solution to the problem of crime and graft.

All this seems clear enough. What is less easy to understand is the empirical basis of the cynical belief that human behaviour is basically so self-centred, so invariably oriented towards personal gain, that no real prospect of behavioural reform actually exists. To talk of any code of ethics is, in this view, a waste of time. Or worse.

Is this cynicism justified? It is hard to see this view as empirically established given the enormous variety of behavioural modes across the world. Some avenues of corruption are thoroughly used in one country, occasionally tried in others, and rarely utilized in still others. Since it is hard to find any generic explanation of these differences (why, for example, a practice shunned in Switzerland may be much used in Italy), we have to look at the pervasive cultural influences on behaviour patterns.

The issue of behavioural reform in the context of preventing corruption relates to the general question of behavioural variations in different cultures and traditions. There is, in fact, plenty of evidence from many spheres of economic, political and social behaviour that different constraints play varying roles in shaping human behaviour. It is also clear that while rules of acceptable behaviour vary, a group that may be quite unmoved by one set of rules may still follow another. Even criminals bent on making money typically follow rules of 'good' gang behaviour, and 'honour among thieves' is not just empty rhetoric. There is very little empirical ground for thoroughgoing scepticism regarding the use of norms.[17] Indeed, the cynical belief that nothing can be changed only replaced high-minded sentimentalism with low-minded sentimentalism – a good example of mushy prejudice masquerading as hard-headed realism.

Perhaps the sceptics in Italy are partly worried by the possibility that the talk of deontological codes may weaken the vigour and speed with which needed institutional reforms are carried out. Certainly, the organization of the economy and establishing rules governing the connection between business and politics demands legal and institutional attention, and attempts at working from that end must not be slackened in the hope of 'behavioural reform'. Indeed, the institutional reforms and behavioural codes have to be seen as complementary to each other, and each can reinforce the other very substantially.

An important issue in behavioural change relates to the influence of modes of conduct of high-ranked public servants and political leaders. This is one of the challenges with which Italy is much concerned right now. The sense of cynicism that pervades a society when it is generally thought that high-placed leaders are pursuing private or sectarian gains from corrupt practices can be deeply demoralizing. It can also profoundly affect the behaviour modes the society finds generally acceptable or unacceptable.

Writing in China in 122 BC, the authors of *Hui-nan Tzu* put the problem thus:

> If the measuring line is true then the wood will be straight, not because one makes a special effort, but because that which it is 'ruled' by makes it so. In the same way if the ruler is sincere and upright, then honest officials will serve in his government and scoundrels will go into hiding, but if the ruler is not upright, then evil men will have their way and loyal men will retire to seclusion.[18]

This piece of ancient wisdom remains as relevant today as it was two thousand years ago.

Organized crime, functional roles and business norms

I now move to the second question related to the hold of corruption and crime. There are social functions that a strong-armed organization like the Mafia can perform in relatively primitive parts of the economy, in supporting mutually beneficial transactions. The functional roles of such organizations depend greatly on the actual behavioural modes in the legal and above-the-counter economy. One example is the part played by such organizations in ensuring the enforcement of contracts and deals, as Stefano Zamagni and others have discussed. The market system requires arrangements for implementation, to prevent one contracting party from letting others down. Such enforcement can either come from the law and its implementation, or – alternatively – be based on mutual trust and an implicit sense of obligation.[19] Since the effective reach of the government can be limited and slow in this field, many business transactions proceed on the basis of trust and honour.

When, however, the standards of market ethics are not yet well established, and feelings of business trust are not well developed, an outside organization can deal with the breach and provide a socially valued service in the form of strong-armed enforcement. An organization like the Mafia can play a useful functional role here, and this can be particularly important in pre-capitalist economies being drawn rapidly into capitalist transactions. Depending on the nature of the interrelations, enforcement of this type may end up being useful for different parties, many of which have no interest at all in corruption or crime. Each contracting partly may simply need 'assurance' that the other economic agents are also doing the appropriate thing.[20]

The part played by strong-armed organizations to generate such 'assurance' depends on the absence of behavioural codes that would reduce the need for such external enforcement. The enforcing function of extra-legal organizations would shrink with an increase in trusting the trust-generating behaviour. The complementarity between behavioural norms and institutional reform can thus be very close indeed. This is a very general issue to consider in dealing with the hold of the Mafia, especially in some backward parts of the economy.

My purpose here is, obviously, not to defend the Mafia. Its role in corruption, murder and other crimes makes it one of the major scourges in modern Italy and elsewhere. But we have to understand the economic basis of the influence of the Mafia by supplementing the recognition of the power of guns and bombs with an understanding of some of the economic activities that make the Mafia a functionally relevant part of the economy. That functional attraction would cease as and when the combined influence of legal enforcement of contracts and behavioural conformity related to mutual trust and normative codes make the Mafia's role in this field quite redundant. There is thus a general connection between the emergence of business norms and the hold of organized crime in rapidly developing, but still partly primitive, economies.

Concluding remarks

I shall not try to summarize this chapter, but will comment on a few of the central issues. First, I have argued that behavioural codes can be quite important for economic organization in general. The importance of moral codes is not contradicted in any way by Adam Smith's pointer to the fact that our 'regard to our own interest' provides adequate motivation for exchange. Smith's butcher–brewer–baker argument is concerned (1) directly with exchange only (not production or distribution), and (2) only with the motivational aspect of exchange (not its organizational and behavioural aspects).

Secondly, successful operation of an exchange economy depends on mutual trust and implicit norms. When these behavioural modes are plentiful, it is easy to overlook their role. But when they have to be cultivated, that lacuna can be a major barrier to economic success. This can be illustrated by (1) the development problems of the Third World, (2) problems of economic reform in the Second World, and (3) variations in productivity and corruptibility in the First World. A basic code of good business behaviour is a bit like oxygen – we take an interest in its presence only when it is absent.

Thirdly, the importance of behavioural codes in the arrangement and performance of production can be illustrated by the contrasting experiences of different economies, for example the remarkable experience of Japanese economic development. The productive advantages of going beyond the pure pursuit of profit can be understood in different ways. To some extent, this question relates to the failure of profit-based market allocation in dealing with 'public goods'. The important connection to note is that in a very real sense the success of a firm can itself be seen as a public good – the fruit of success is shared by the different parties involved in the firm rather than being parcelled out in neat little packets of individual rewards strictly related to individual contributions.

Fourthly, the hold of organized crime (like the influence of the Mafia) in some economies relates partly to the underdevelopment of business norms and codes on which economic transactions depend, since that underdevelopment gives strong-armed organizations a functional role that they can exploit to build the basis of their power. Making the functional role redundant will contribute to fighting organized crime – a battle that calls for an economic as well as a policing response.

Finally, codes of behaviour in a particular society may be hard to change, but there is little empirical basis for taking them to be immutable. Our behaviour patterns depend much on the emulation of others and on acting according to norms that seem standard in the society in which we live. In this respect, the current Italian – and to some extent the Japanese – emphasis on eliminating corrupt behaviour on the part of highly visible business and political leaders seems particularly appropriate. While there is reason for pessimism about emulated misbehaviour, there are grounds for optimism about imitated honour. If actual behaviour depends on norms, norms too depend on actual behaviour.

Notes

1. I am grateful for research facilities at STICERD at the London School of Economics, where this paper was written.
2. Adam Smith, (1776 republished 1910), vol. I, p. 13.
3. In this context I shall take the liberty of drawing on my talk to the Anti-Mafia Commission of the Italian Parliament on 15 May 1993 (to be published, in Italian, by the Commission).
4. I have discussed Smith's views in more detail in Sen (1987, 1993a). See also Patricia H. Werhane (1991) and Emma Rothschild (1992).
5. Adam Smith (revised edition 1790, reprinted 1975), p. 191.
6. Smith (1790, 1975), pp. 190–92.
7. Smith (1790, 1975), p. 189.
8. I have tried to discuss this issue in Sen (1986).
9. In this sense, the codes of business and professional behaviour are parts of the productive capital of a society. On this question, see Armando Massarenti and Antonio Da Re (1991).
10. See Sen (1993b).
11. Ronald Dore (1983, 1987). See also Robert Wade (1990).
12. Recently, Eiko Ikegami (1991) has pointed to the importance of the traditional concern with 'honour' – a kind of generalization of the Samurai code - as a crucial modifier of business and economic motivation.

13. *The Wall Street Journal*, 30 January 1989, p. 1.
14. Karl Marx (with F. Engels), (1845–6, English translation, 1947); Richard Henry Tawney, (1926); Max Weber (1930).
15. The classic treatment of public goods was provided by Paul A. Samuelson (1954).
16. See the proceedings of the conference on Economics and Criminality in Rome in May 1993, organized by the Italian Parliament's Anti-Mafia Commission – Luciano Violante (1993). My paper to that conference (On 'Corruption and Organized Crime') addresses, in greater detail, some of the issues discussed in this section, with particular reference to the Italian situation.
17. On this see Sen (1984) and the references cited therein.
18. English translation from Alatas (1980); see also Klitgaard (1988).
19. For general analyses of the role of trust, see the essays included in Diego Gambetta (1987).
20. On this see Sen (1967, 1987).

References

Alatas, S.H. (1980), *The Sociology of Corruption*, Singapore: Times Books.
Aoki, M. (1989), *Information, Incentive and Bargaining in the Japanese Economy*, Cambridge: Cambridge University Press.
Dore, R. (1983), 'Goodwill and the Spirit of Market Capitalism', *British Journal of Sociology*, **34**, 459–82.
Dore, R. (1987), *Taking Japan Seriously: A Confucian Perspective on Leading Economic Issues*, Stanford: Stanford University Press.
Gambetta, D. (ed.) (1987), *Trust and Agency*, Oxford: Blackwell.
Ikegami, E. (1991), 'The Logic of Cultural Change: Honor, State-Making, and the Samurai', mimeographed, Department of Sociology, Yale University.
Klitgaard, R. (1988), *Controlling Corruption*, Berkeley: University of California Press.
Marx, K. (with F. Engels) (1845–6, 1947), *The German Ideology*, New York: International Publishers.
Massarenti, A. and Da Re, A. (1991), *L'Etica de Applicare*, Milano: Il Sole 24 Ore Libri.
Morishima, M. (1982), *Why Has Japan 'Succeeded'? Western Technology and Japanese Ethos*, Cambridge: Cambridge University Press.
Rothschild, E. (1992), 'Adam Smith and Conservative Economics', *Economic History Review*, **45**, 74–96.
Samuelson, P.A. (1954), 'The Pure Theory of Public Expenditure', *Review of Economics and Statistics*, **36**, 387–9.
Sen, A.K. (1967), 'Isolation, Assurance and the Social Rate of Discount', *Quarterly Journal of Economics*, **81**, 112–24.
Sen, A.K. (1984), *Resources, Values and Development*, Oxford: Blackwell.
Sen, A.K. (1986), 'Adam Smith's Prudence', in Lal, S. and Stewart, F. (eds), *Theory and Reality in Development*, London: Macmillan.
Sen, A.K. (1987), *On Ethics and Economics*, Oxford: Blackwell.
Sen, A.K. (1993a), 'Does Business Ethics Make Economic Sense?', *Business Ethics Quarterly*, **3**, 45–63.
Sen, A.K. (1993b), 'The Economics of Life and Death', *Scientific American*, May, 18–25.
Smith, A. (1776, 1910), *An Inquiry into the Nature and Causes of the Wealth of Nations*, London: Dent.
Smith, A. (1790, 1975), *The Theory of Moral Sentiments* (edited by D. Raphael and A. Macfie), Oxford: Clarendon Press.
Tawney, R.H. (1926), *Religion and the Rise of Capitalism*, London: Murray.
Violante, L. (1993), *Economica e Criminalita*, Roma: Camera dei Deputati.
Wade, R. (1990), *Governing the Market*, Princeton: Princeton University Press.
Weber, M. (1930), *The Protestant Ethic and the Spirit of Capitalism*, London: Allen & Unwin.
Werhane, P.H. (1991), *Adam Smith and his Legacy for Modern Capitalism*, New York: Oxford University Press.

3 Some reflections on morality and capitalism
Nigel Lawson

Introduction

Some 15 years ago, towards the end of the unhappy life of the last Labour Government, I contributed to a book of essays published under the somewhat apocalyptic title, *The Coming Confrontation* and sub-titled, *Will the Open Society Survive to 1989?*

I chose as the theme for my own essay what I termed 'The Moral Dimension'. I began by asserting what seemed to me to be a paradox:

> There can by now be no doubt that collectivism has failed. Throughout the nations of the industrialised world, the people are freer and their living standards higher the less far-reaching is the degree of state ownership, direction and control of the economy. Yet, throughout the industrialised world, the frontiers of the state, so far from being rolled back, are almost everywhere being further extended (Lawson, 1978).

After examining various possible reasons for this paradox, I concluded that the principal explanation lay in the fact that:

> It is the moral dimension that lies at the heart of the matter. For man is a moral animal, and no political or economic order can long survive except on a moral base ... (Yet) the apologists of capitalism have hoped to win the day on the merits of its fruits, and have unwisely allowed the moral dimension to go by default. The apologists of the barren tree of socialism, by contrast, have played the moral card for all it is worth – and a good deal more besides (Lawson, 1978).

In this chapter I shall be revisiting this topic and – in the light of ten years' experience as a Minister – be reflecting further on the relationship between capitalism and morality.

For the avoidance of doubt, incidentally, I use the term 'capitalism' to describe an economic order based on free markets and private property – not, let me add, in some theoretical or ideal sense, but in the only way in which any system should be judged, namely as we know it in the real world. And by 'the world' I do indeed mean the world – the capitalism of Japan, for example, as much as that of the United States.

Much has changed since 1978. The seemingly inexorable extension of the frontiers of the state has been emphatically reversed. Throughout the Western world, and notably since the coming into office of the Thatcher Government in the UK in 1979 and the Reagan Administration in the USA in 1981, capitalism has appeared to be in the ascendent and socialism in retreat. Nor has this trend been confined to the Western world. During the course of the 1980s much of the developing world, too, came belatedly to recognize the benefits, and adopt the policies, of the market economy. As an intermittent attender at meetings of Commonwealth Finance Ministers, I can vouch for a quite remarkable change over that period.

But the most dramatic development has been the great changes in Central and Eastern Europe, where the collapse of communism and the command economy has revealed a landscape of economic failure, poverty and environmental degradation on a scale that few had believed possible. It is perhaps not surprising to find that the most passionate supporters of the capitalist market economy today are to be found among the ablest of the new leaders of these countries. Nor, incidentally, are recent events in China without interest.

There is nothing particularly surprising about the unrivalled practical success of market capitalism. It is not surprising that people give of their best in a climate of freedom, within a legal and institutional framework of order and justice. Nor is it in any way surprising that the rational decisions needed to make a modern economy even half-way efficient can be taken only by a multiplicity of decision-makers armed with the knowledge provided by a myriad of market prices.

What is surprising is that, despite all this, and the important events of the past decade, which have led even the British Labour Party to reconsider its commitment to socialist egalitarianism and hostility to the market economy, the 'atmosphere of hostility to capitalism' which Schumpeter remarked upon some 50 years ago is still so pervasive.

And the reason for this is clear. While its material success, and its demonstrable superiority over all known alternative economic systems, is no longer open to question, capitalism is still widely seen as morally suspect.

(In parentheses, I must confess that I find myself distinctly uneasy about the tendency towards the collectivization of morality; in which moral censure is reserved for governments and politico-economic systems, with individuals seen as innocent victims. We would do better to stick to the traditional idea of morality as a matter of individual personal responsibility.)

Be that as it may, why should capitalism be seen as morally suspect, given its unrivalled and proven ability to improve living standards and eliminate large-scale poverty, and its unique harmony with the political virtues of freedom and democracy?

In part, the explanation clearly lies in sloppy thinking. There is a frequent tendency to contrast, consciously or subconsciously, the market capitalism we know, with all the faults and flaws we see around us, with some ideal economic order which would, almost by definition, be free of these imperfections. In fact, of course, in an imperfect world, the only valid comparison is with other systems as they actually operate (or have operated) in practice.

Similarly, there is a parochial predilection to blame the moral failings of man, which – not surprisingly – are evident throughout the world, on the nature of the politico-economic system in place where the critic happens to reside.

But in the case of the alleged moral failings of capitalism, it has to be conceded that there is rather more to it than that.

Morality, as most people see it, is a matter partly of motivation and partly of outcomes. And market capitalism is widely seen as defective in both respects.

Self-interest

So far as motivation is concerned, it is seen as a system based on self-interest, the very antithesis of morality – for what is the essence of a moral code if it is not the curbing of selfishness and self-gratification?

As for the outcome, while the population as a whole might benefit from capitalism, that benefit is shared to an unequal extent that many feel *ipso facto* immoral.

It is these two characteristics, self-interest and inequality, that largely explain the alleged moral deficiencies of capitalism. Let me take them each in turn.

A regard for one's self-interest is a prominent feature in the make-up of almost all mankind. It is not the only feature, but it is a uniquely powerful one. Moreover, it is hard to see how, without it, a large-scale free society could possibly be governable. A socialist or statist government, besides its apparatus of restrictions and controls, creates, through the tax system and grants of one kind and another, inducements designed to encourage those forms of economic behaviour it believes to be desirable. But unless people sought to advance their self-interest, these inducements would clearly be ineffective.

The characteristic of market capitalism is not that it alone is based on the idea of channelling self-interest for the greater good – not that there is anything wrong with that. It is rather that it is a unique mechanism for doing so directly, with the least interposition of government.

Why, then, is market capitalism alone thought to be based on the allegedly morally disreputable concept of the pursuit of self-interest?

Partly, perhaps, because Adam Smith, more than 200 years ago, was so disarmingly honest about it. Those who seek to commend a politico-economic system are expected to be decently hypocritical, and to flatter their audience by speaking in loftier tones.

But it is also partly because, whereas capitalism is customarily discussed in terms of the motives of the governed, socialism is usually considered in terms of the motives of those in government.

Even that, however, is very much a distinction without a difference. There is little practical evidence that politicians and bureaucrats are wholly altruistic beings, on a higher moral plane than vulgar businessmen – as that admirable television documentary, *Yes, Prime Minister*, has well illustrated.

It is true that in a country such as ours, where pecuniary corruption is rare, there is the distinction that, whereas businessmen seek financial reward, politicians seek votes. But that is no basis for according moral superiority to a system in which more decisions are taken by politicians and bureaucrats, and fewer by businessmen and ordinary people.

Moreover, there are important positive moral arguments in favour of market capitalism, quite apart from the freedom and liberty on which it is based, and the beneficent results to which it has led, to which I have already alluded.

In the first place, there is the extent to which it gives greater freedom than other systems – albeit still within strict limits, set by the rule of law – for the peaceful pursuit of self-interest, in practice that means the natural desire of men and women to benefit not merely themselves but also their family, in particular their children.

To my mind this is a vitally important extension, not to be dismissed as genetic selfishness. When parents neglect their children (or worse), as in recent well-publicized 'home alone' cases and the like, we do not regard this as a lack of genetic selfishness, but with horror as morally unacceptable behaviour. Subordinating one's own personal interest to that of one's family is not the beginning and end of altruism, to be sure; but it *is* the beginning, as it is the foundation and cradle of social behaviour.

The family, which looms large in the scheme of market capitalism, is not only the foundation of a stable society, but an important bulwark against tyranny – as, of course, is the institution of private property, the more widely spread the better. Hence the infallible rule that tyrannies always seek to weaken, if not destroy, the family. Jung Chang, in her remarkable book *Wild Swans*, shows particularly poignantly how Maoist communism felt obliged to wage war on the family loyalties so deeply rooted in Chinese culture, and quotes a line in a song much heard on the eve of the devastating Cultural Revolution: 'Father is close, and Mother is close, but neither is as close as Chairman Mao'.

Another key feature of market capitalism is the private sector, non-monopolistic, firm. Capitalism is sometimes portrayed either as monopolistic exploitation or an unattractive competitive jungle, where the values of co-operation are lost in a free-for-all. What this overlooks is that the private sector firm itself provides a model of effective co-operation, which the preoccupation of economists (inasmuch as they are interested in the firm at all) with the company as a single corporate personality, seeking to maximize its profits as it lurches along its U-shaped cost curve, should not be allowed to obscure.

These two institutions, the family and the firm, come together, of course, in that much-derided corporate entity, the family business. While more important at earlier stages of development than later stages, and in some cultures more than in others, I suspect that the value of the family business and the culture it represents has been insufficiently recognized.

Egalitarianism
But while the misguided moral critique of market capitalism as irredeemably selfish has been allowed to acquire considerable resonance, an even more powerful ground for moral disfavour has been the inequality to which it leads.

Yet in these terms, the closer the charge is examined the less impressive it appears. There is clearly no principle of equality that has any conceivable merit. Equality in misery is of no value to anyone. And equality of opportunity – an admirable aspiration, provided it is sought by levelling up rather than levelling down – is clearly a different matter altogether. Indeed, given the widely different capacities of different individuals, not to mention the inescapable caprice of chance, the one thing that genuine equality of opportunity can be guaranteed to produce is inequality of outcome.

Nor, incidentally, is it clear whether equality should be considered within the context of the nation and society in which we live, or in the wider context of the world as a whole. Even in the narrower context, it is doubtful if there can be more than a tiny minority of eccentrics who wish to see a society in which absolute equality is the rule. Yet once it is accepted that there must be inequality, the principle of equality (if there ever was one) has been abandoned, and we are left not with morality but with something that looks rather like an amalgam of aesthetics and envy.

Not that absolute equality, or anything approaching it, is possible anyway (which is one good reason why it has never existed anywhere, at any time). For one thing, there is more than one dimension of equality: it is not simply a matter of income and wealth. In particular, the closer to pecuniary equality a government seeks to move, the greater the coercive powers needed to achieve this, and the greater the inequality of power between government and governed.

Moreover, absolute equality, even in the sense in which it is theoretically attainable, must of necessity lead to misery. If there is to be no greater reward for work or saving or effort of any kind than is received by those who decline to work or save or make any effort, then remarkably little work, saving or effort will be undertaken. This is not simply an elementary economic proposition. It is also intimately connected with a more robust moral sentiment: that associated with equity and desert. If two people are working at the same job, with equal skill, and one chooses to work overtime while the other does not, failure to pay the former more would be seen as not merely self-defeating but grossly inequitable.

It is true that large disparities in rates of pay can give rise, particularly when hyped up by the populist press, to storms of apparent moral outrage. But this has nothing to do with attachment to any principle of equality. People do not expect some third division nonentity to be paid the same as Eric Cantona, or a chorus girl the same as Pavarotti. While we are all equal under the law and in the sight of God, we are not all equally good footballers or singers; and people well understand that pay relates to performance, as measured in the market-place, rather than to moral worth. Simple envy aside, the outrage is based either on ignorance of the reason for the high pay, or on disapproval of the individual receiving it – or the way he makes his money, or both.

Not that any specific inequality is necessarily justified even in economic terms: it may well not be. The argument for market capitalism is not that it is infallible – no human construction could possibly be infallible – but that it is superior to any other politico-economic order.

For these reasons, the egalitarian argument is usually couched in terms not of equality *tout court* but rather those of *more* equality. One problem with this, however, is the *insatiability* of egalitarianism. Once the legitimacy of egalitarianism is accepted, however much equality there is, the cry will always be for more of it. If and when taxes come down, it will be held that the worse off should be the beneficiaries: when they go up, it will be held that it is the better off that should bear the burden. That is how the UK ended up, at the close of the 1970s, with the absurd top rates of income tax of 75 per cent on earnings and 98 per cent on savings income.

The Government of which I was a member felt that this was far too high, and I myself played a part in reversing the process. I recall vividly how this was characterized by my egalitarian critics as 'handouts for the rich' and, as such, self-evidently immoral. The concept that egalitarianism might have gone too far was not one that they could accept.

It is the combination of the insatiability of egalitarianism with the impossibility of achieving equality that causes the elevation of equality into the touchstone of political morality to be a recipe for maximizing discontent. In a sense, indeed, it is positively immoral. A moment ago I referred to envy. Anthony Crosland, in the original (1956) edition of his important book *The Future of Socialism*, openly discussed the necessity for the Labour Party to base its appeal on envy – although in later editions he prudently abridged this section. Even so, in his 1975 Fabian Tract, *Social Democracy in Europe*, he was obliged to admit that egalitarianism was not primarily concerned with improving the lot of the less well off: '... the argument for more equality is based not on any direct material gain for the poor, but on the claims of social and natural justice.'

Natural justice it cannot be; and 'social justice' is simply a term dreamed up to mean the same as, but to sound more impressive than, greater equality – rendering that part of his assertion an empty tautology.

Nevertheless, Crosland's claim is useful in making the distinction, which as an honest man he was obliged to do, between equality and the relief of poverty. Market capitalism is the best system ever devised for the avoidance of large-scale poverty and for enabling the poor to improve their lot. But what it manifestly does not ensure is the elimination of poverty altogether.

That is why the voters rightly expect of any government that it should operate a social security system for the relief of poverty, and why all governments, however wedded to market capitalism, in practice do so. There are obviously a number of practical questions involved in this. It is not merely a case of how poverty is to be defined (certainly not in terms of the average wage), but also whether relief should be targeted or part of some universal benefit (overwhelmingly the former, I believe), whether other dimensions should be taken into account (age certainly should, and the 1985 social security reforms erred in this respect); whether relief for the unemployed poor should be linked to some form of workfare (I believe it should), and so on.

But the key point is this. So far from making a case against market capitalism, the existence of an underclass is a challenge to find a means of minimizing its size and saving those in it from degradation without in any way undermining market capitalism or detracting from the benefits that system has proved itself to be uniquely capable of providing. Just as the sensible successful businessman who seeks to help those less fortunate will do so not by changing the way he runs his business but by applying part of his personal wealth to philanthropy, so the wise government will best help the poor not by interfering with the market but by creating a well-designed social security safety net alongside it.

I have referred more than once to the success of market capitalism – a success that is now recognized even by the more thoughtful members of the Labour Party. For example Professor Raymond Plant, *inter alia* Chairman of the Labour Party's working party on electoral systems, wrote recently that:

> Both the intellectual and political case against command economies and central economic planning has been won. The intellectual debate since Reagan, Thatcher and the changes in Eastern Europe is no longer about central economic planning or the case for the market but much more about the range of social and political institutions within which markets are embedded, the scope and purposes of these institutions, and their relationship to the market economy (Plant, 1992).

Market capitalism, to give it its proper name (or, more fully, democratic market capitalism), has, compared with all other known systems, scored on every front: freedom, opportunity, protection of the environment, the living standards of the average family. In this last context, it has proved itself to be a more favourable environment for economic growth than any other the world has known.

Growth
But is it the case, as some argue, that it is only the fact of economic growth that makes market capitalism politically acceptable? The argument here is, essentially, that the unequal distribution of wealth is acceptable, and the system seen

as having legitimacy, only because it is in principle open to anyone to improve their position without disadvantaging others – since the possibility of growth, which market capitalism is best able to realize, ensures that economic change is not a zero-sum game.

Thus when (the argument continues) the Malthusian nightmare becomes reality, as in a finite world it must, and growth comes to a full stop (not to say goes into reverse), market capitalism will cease to be morally acceptable: the whole basis of its legitimacy will have disappeared.

Strictly speaking, it is no part of government's job to seek to bring about the maximum practicable growth in recorded GNP. The government's job, in the economic field, is to create the legal and institutional framework required for market capitalism to thrive, together with the other essential element of the required framework – needed, incidentally, for social as well as economic reasons – namely, price stability.

Whatever the case for government intervention in the working of the capitalist market economy for social purposes, to intervene in order to boost economic growth is doubly perverse – first because, as I have just maintained, growth as such should not be an objective of government policy; and secondly because experience has shown that the capitalist market economy is (for good reasons) better able than government action to produce growth.

The point here is that the government's responsibility is to create the conditions in which individuals can generate growth, if that is what they desire, in the way in which they desire it. And they surely do and will continue to do so, even though the form may change. Despite Christianity's uneasiness with market capitalism, it was Pope John Paul II who declared that creativity was the essence of man, which implies the need for the freedom to create; and it is man's creativity which produces growth.

Certainly, if and when the combination of rising population and finite resources leads to an end to growth and to a world of falling material living standards, discontent with market capitalism may well increase – as indeed would discontent with any other economic system that happened to prevail at the time. The extent of the discontent might depend, of course, on the pace of the decline and the extent to which (as a result of technological progress) it is accompanied by increasing leisure time which can be spent in ways that make minimal demands on resources.

But it is difficult to see why this should fatally undermine the legitimacy of the capitalist market system. For the essence of the market economy, and its great moral attribute, is voluntarism: the fact that economic transactions are freely undertaken because each side benefits. This would continue to be true even if and when overall growth has ceased.

All this, moreover, is in any case a very long way off. We may live in a world of finite resources, but the price mechanism ensures that we respond to scarcity by becoming progressively less wasteful – see, for example, the steadily diminishing energy content of output. And, in general, in what is sometimes termed somewhat optimistically 'the information age', the material content of growth appears to be diminishing. Only a very small portion of the market value of a pop video, for example, is attributable to its visible plastic form.

For all of these reasons, it would be the height of folly to doubt the legitimacy of market capitalism in the world in which we live because of the problems that would arise – problems, incidentally, that would bedevil far more than market capitalism – were the Malthusian nightmare to become, one day, reality.

Conclusion

Throughout modern history, market capitalism has sought to rest its case on its material success – a relative success which, over the past five years, events in Central and Eastern Europe have shown in a particularly telling light. Socialism, by contrast, has been forced by practical failure onto the high ground of morality.

Perhaps we could leave it there. Perhaps we should adapt the description of the Roundheads and Cavaliers in *1066 And All That*, and accept that capitalism is right but repulsive, whereas socialism is wrong but romantic. But I would not feel comfortable in doing so. Success, which is inevitably incomplete anyway, will sooner or later always be taken for granted, and then the moral assault, if unanswered, will gain ground. At the very least, if we are to live within a market capitalist system, it is unsatisfactory that we should have doubts about its moral foundations. One or two recent speeches, even by some members of the present Government, betray a worrying insecurity in this context.

In this essay I have not sought to enumerate the moral values that tend, in practice, to be associated rather more with democratic market capitalism than with any other known politico-economic order: such attributes as probity, integrity, honesty, fair-dealing, trust, respect for others (including their property) and the like – still less have I sought to discuss whether these values are adopted for their own sake or because experience teaches us that honesty is the best policy (both elements are clearly, it seems to me, present).

In particular, I have dealt only cursorily with the profound connection between market capitalism and the moral value of freedom and voluntarism. I have done so partly because I have become increasingly aware over the years that there is no single moral value which can serve as the sole foundation for a political, economic or social system, or for the conduct of personal life, and that the search for one is a wild goose chase. And I have done it partly because I felt it more important to examine the alleged moral defects of market capitalism.

It is obvious that I write from a particular perspective, which may not be universally shared. Morality, in any case, is a field in which it is particularly easy for intelligent people to reach divergent conclusions. But at least, in seeking to repudiate the moral critique of capitalism, and to suggest that it should not be held responsible for the moral imperfection of man, I do not need to win my case. For even a stand-off in the moral dimension is enough to allow market capitalism's undoubted superiority in the world of practical achievement to win the day.

Bibliography

Crosland, C.A.R. (1975), *Social Democracy in Europe*, London: Fabian Society.

Lawson, N. (1978), 'The Moral Dimension', in *The Coming Confrontation: Twelve Essays by Different Authors*, London: Institute of Economic Affairs.

Plant, R. (1992), *Autonomy, Social Rights and Distributive Justice*, London: IEA Health and Welfare Unit.

Schumpeter, J.A. (1943), *Capitalism, Socialism and Democracy*, London: George Allen & Unwin.

4 The ethics of unemployment and Mafia capitalism

John S. Flemming

Introduction

In this chapter I address four related themes all involving economics and ethics within the framework of mainstream economic analysis. I have, therefore, first to demonstrate that this framework admits ethical consideration before going on to examine three cases: Keynesian unemployment in industrial economies in recession; similar but more extreme phenomena in formerly centrally planned economies in transition; and wider aspects of the economy of the 'wild east'.

The first two applications relate to the ethical challenge of unemployment; if the evil of employment should be contained how should it be done? Are the attitudes and values giving rise to relatively inflexible money wages themselves evil? Might their partial erosion actually make things worse? How would policy be different if it were optimized subject to the constraints of those attitudes and the institutional rigidities they support? In Eastern Europe the problem is more acute and the dangers of inappropriate policies even greater.

I argue that liberalization alone is liable to lead to a steep fall in the market-clearing real wage in reforming economies and that if the fall is restricted, as by a minimum wage, unemployment is liable to occur. If reform is to make most people better off, as should be possible and is necessary to consolidate support for the process, liberalization of trade and prices needs to be complemented by temporary general employment subsidies or tariff protection designed to make liberalized prices adjust only gradually to the new equilibration.

Finally the role of profits in the process of equilibration, the parasites they attract, the limitations of the justification for corruption as an application of the logic of the market, and the importance of tax compliance for the transition (and after) are discussed.

The framework

But first I must establish the consistency of an economics conventionally described as postulating selfishness with a concern for the broader social effects of economic policy which, to be relevant in a democracy, almost certainly requires that, as voters, citizen-consumers reflect a concern for the welfare of others. Of course some concern with the welfare of the elderly is a consequence of rational foresight – we will all draw pensions if we survive long enough – but the extent even of what remains of the welfare state is difficult to rationalize on this basis alone, that is in the absence of many individuals who are altruistically concerned about the welfare of many other individuals.

At the same time conventional economics, and particularly the case for decentralized market systems, does depend to a considerable extent on the postulate of selfishness. The two requirements are not, however, very difficult to reconcile – a reconciliation that shifts the focus of economic ethics from the market-place to the political arena which I shall present in two stages.

Consider first a society consisting of identical individuals faced with identical opportunities. If the technology to which they have access involves diminishing returns to each individual's activity of any type, they will all do the same thing and enjoy the same living standard and there would be no scope either for trade or for voluntary charitable transfers – though there might be scope for exchanging gifts as expressions of affection or as part of religious or similar rituals such as the celebration of birthdays. Ethics would also be involved in respecting each other's property.

Only the voluntary transfers would, if they existed, challenge an explanation of production and consumption based on selfishness, and their symmetry would be consistent with a mutually beneficial trade in esteem and affection based on implicit contracts.

A minor modification to the assumption about technology would lead to specialization by functions, such as ploughman, herdswoman and potter, and generate trade in products. Given the assumption of identical talents, specialization would be arbitrary, and free entry would ensure that each profession yielded the same level of satisfaction in equilibrium. Again selfishness would suffice to explain all economic activities and exchanges even if people were not selfish in the sense that, faced by inequality and individuals in want, they would make voluntary unrequited transfers.

In order to make this an operational possibility we have to generate some inequality – possibly quite a lot. Selfishness is, after all, a matter of degree, as is altruism – which only in its extreme form requires the placing of priority on the satisfaction of others over one's own satisfaction. Ethical and general altruism – I work solely for your good while you work solely for mine – is not only implausible but not even particularly attractive and is certainly inefficient. I can work more effectively for myself than for you – and vice versa – if we both have similar talents. But if selfishness is a matter of degree, so is the amount of inequality required to lead its limitations to manifest themselves.

If I attach half as much weight to any one else's satisfaction as my own I will only make unrequited transfers to people I believe to be so poor as to get twice as much benefit from a pound of expenditure as I would – and that may mean people with less than half my income. A society made up of such people would only reveal their limited selfishness if it generated a range of incomes in which the highest was more than twice the lowest.

Even then we should not expect an organized society to rely on individual charity. If everyone in a society is unselfish they all feel happier when its poorest member is better fed. Transfers from the rich to the poor need to be co-ordinated, and even incompletely selfish people will be tempted to enjoy the knowledge that the poor are fed without making their own contributions – others' contributions suffice to reduce inequality below the critical point for direct giving. Thus an element of coercion is required, or rather assurance that everyone else is making their contribution too.

If random inequality of endowments were introduced into the otherwise homogeneous society we have been describing, there would be unanimous support for a scheme of limited compulsory redistribution – perhaps better not labelled coercion. Given the redistribution thus achieved through taxation, individuals would act as if selfish, the limited nature of their selfishness having been expressed through their support for redistributive taxation.

This is obviously a particularly simple case, but it suffices to make my first point: a society in which all individual economic activity, choices of training, profession, goods, saving and so on, are explicable in selfish terms is not incompatible at all with a citizenry whose concern for others is reflected in their having voted for some form of welfare state that modifies the outcome of their 'as-if-selfish' economic behaviour; no schizophrenia is involved.

Of course in reality some people may be completely selfish – and certainly people differ in the degree of their unselfishness, and thus in their preferences relating to the scale and nature of redistribution and the welfare state. This is the stuff of politics, and I have said that it is in the political arena rather than the market-place that most economic ethics should manifest itself – the exception being the ethics of trust, in mutual exchange and respect for property. It is thus simply false to say that conventional market economies require that *homo economicus* be selfish and unfeeling for others. It is quite sufficient that he give some priority to himself and that his concern for others be reflected in political support for redistributive and regulatory mechanisms within which framework he seeks to maximize his own selfish objectives.

This argument produces a particularly stark conclusion which I would not necessarily endorse. The 'public good' nature, in the technical sense, of the benefits of redistribution of income or wealth makes that a natural function of the state with its machinery of compulsion. No rationalization has been offered for the role of charities or charitable giving in a society with a welfare state. This failure would matter if the purpose were to explain the world, but does nothing to undermine the conclusion that a concern for others expressed at the ballot box is perfectly compatible with apparently (and really) selfish behaviour in the market-place.

Unemployment

It is a simple matter of definition that perfectly flexible wages would ensure continuous clearing of the labour market and thus the absence of unemployment.

The existence of unemployment thus raises several questions:

1. Why are wages at all inflexible?
2. Are the preferences or social institutions that render wages inflexible reprehensible?
3. Would things necessarily be improved by making wages more flexible?
4. How far can appropriate monetary policy reduce unemployment given the inflexibility of money wages?

The late Sir John Hicks distinguished between fix-price and flex-price markets, the latter occurring typically in standardized commodities often traded on one form or another of an auction market (such as the London Metal Exchange). Other goods are either subject to specific negotiated contracts or offered by sellers at specified prices. If the cost of negotiations is to be contained they have to relate to large or repeated transactions. In the repeated case the price at which subsequent deliveries occur is predetermined, but the buyer is also precommitted: cancellation carries a penalty. Where a price is set without the quantity being set the price is usually, and more efficiently, set by the traders on the side of the market where they are less numerous. This usually means the supplier of goods or the buyers of labour – unless employing firms outnumber organized trade unions.

Where prices are set two related questions arise: are they linked to any index during the currency of their setting, and how often are they revised? There is an extensive and inconclusive literature on these questions as they apply to wages.

Among the hypotheses contributing to inflexibility are:

1. Elements of monopoly (working both ways).
2. Elements of social convention.
3. Specific concern with relative pay.
4. Problems and costs of informing people of rapidly changing wages.

In practice it is easier to model aggregate wages not as adjusting infrequently but as adjusting partially, at a finite speed, towards their equilibrium value which, in the case of money wages, depends on what is happening to the money supply at the same time.

If one wants to reduce the social evil of unemployment one could try to erode the features accounting for their incomplete adjustment. I shall suggest that this would be an unwise course on which to embark, unless one were confident of complete success, as a modest increase in the speed with which wages adjust could actually increase the average level of unemployment.

The alternative is to conduct monetary policy so as to minimize unemployment given the speed with which wages adjust – bearing in mind, however, the possibility that the adjustment speed is itself a reflection of the context of wage bargaining – including monetary policy and the incidence of unemployment.

First I should explain how, on the assumption of a fixed money supply, greater wage flexibility could actually increase the instability of employment. The basic point is that prices depend to some extent on nominal wages. If wages adjust more quickly to unemployment, this will be built into rational expectations in the aftermath of a deflationary shock to aggregate demand. If wages are expected to fall more rapidly, so too will prices be expected to fall faster, translating a given nominal interest rate into a higher real interest rate and depressing demand further. Of course the nominal interest rate might fall – but that would only happen to short rates if either the price level or the level of output had fallen – reducing the demand for money. Given the money wage, any fall in prices raises the real wage and – in an essentially neoclassical model – unemployment. Thus the effect of less sticky money wages is to increase the impact effect of deflationary shocks if the authorities pursue a fixed money supply rule.[1]

Of course more flexible wages, as defined here in terms of adjustment speed, mean that the economy reverts more rapidly to its equilibrium in the aftermath of a shock. But this is at best a mixed blessing: what is the net effect of amplifying the impact of disturbances while accelerating subsequent adjustment to them? Obviously this will depend on the details of one's model and its parameters, but it is certainly quite possible that the net effect is to increase the variance of employment around its natural rate.[2]

Thus any attack on the social institutions and attitudes that might be blamed for making wages inflexible, and thus for the evil of unstable employment, rests on rather weak foundations.

Although perhaps at first surprising, the proposition that more of something that sounds, at least economically, 'good', like wage flexibility, may actually be harmful, should not in fact come as a surprise. The general theory of the second best tells us that reducing one obstacle to the best possible state of affairs – in this case wage inflexibility – can only be relied upon to be an improvement if all the other requirements of the optimum are already in place.

In this case, by assumption, all other markets worked perfectly, but we assumed an arbitrarily fixed money supply rule. The ethical citizen should not necessarily attack his neighbours' attitudes and beliefs, but rather advocate a different monetary policy. I am not arguing here that all unemployment is attributable to bad monetary policy – merely that much of what is blamed on sticky wages is more properly attributed to the monetary authorities.

What should they do to accommodate the fact that wages are sticky while not providing inflationary cover for arbitrary wage increases? The answer is not simple, particularly if, as is realistic, they do not know with confidence the equilibrium level of unemployment – which may in any case evolve randomly. They could try to stabilize unemployment at any particular level; if that policy were to generate accelerating inflation they would know they had set too low a target level and could raise it. But inflation has its own dynamics and the error could prove costly, as to lower inflation expectations, once built up, might take a considerable period of extra unemployment. Thus we face a difficult trade-off between employment stability and price or inflation stability. This trade-off is quite different from that represented by the famous Phillips curve, relating to an alleged relationship between the rate of money wage increase and unemployment, and is not reliably improved by increased wage flexibility.

Eastern Europe
Unemployment in Western Europe has, since 1970, exceeded that in the United States, where it has risen little since the early post-war decades. In the European Community it averaged 10 per cent in the 1980s and is currently at a slightly higher cyclical peak.

The reforming economies of Eastern Europe fall into three categories; some, like Russia, where measured output has fallen by over 30 per cent, still report pretty meaningless registered unemployment of around 1 per cent. A few others, like the Czech and Slovak Republics, have unemployment around US and Western European levels. More typical and realistic, however, are rates in the mid-teens and still rising – though possibly slowing. Was unemployment approaching 20 per cent an inevitable consequence of economic liberalization? What remedies should the ethical citizen advocate? I should stress that I do not believe that much Eastern European unemployment is Keynesian, but my title was already overloaded. In any case the argument here depends in part on wage flexibility.

Under plausible assumptions about the relevant technology, the effect of the radical changes in effective relative prices consequent upon price and trade liberalization is a collapse in the market-clearing real wage. In an extreme, but not implausible, case it is hard to see what provides any floor to the wage. We know that the distortions in many centrally planned economies were so great that they had plants which actually subtracted value at world prices. Oil in Russia was less than one-tenth of its world price. Some shoddy appliances, produced using a lot of energy and metals, could not be sold on the world market at a price that would cover the cost (at world prices) of the raw materials used in their production – before making any provision for paying for the labour involved.

Unless capable of rapid design and productivity improvement, such an enterprise, which would be unprofitable at any wage or exchange rate, will and should close. The question is at what wage those losing jobs there can be absorbed elsewhere. This obviously depends in the short run on the scope for them to contribute to additional production on the equipment already in place, which is likely to be inflexible. It is not absurd to suggest that beyond a certain point the contribution of extra hands should be zero – or even less if they get in the way. Moreover, if those employed in the value-subtracting activities had similar skills to those in the still value-adding ones, competition in the labour market would ensure that the wage of those still employed was no higher than that acceptable to the unemployed – which would reflect income support or subsistence employment opportunities. Such a situation, which has not emerged openly in Eastern Europe, is obviously unsatisfactory, even though the high profits possibly associated with it might in due course fuel rapid investment, industrial adjustment and reabsorption of labour.

Economists like policy changes that make everyone better off (a Pareto improvement) and elementary welfare economics suggests that such policies should be available in the case of the severely distorted economies bequeathed by decades of central planning. Such policies, if they can be identified, should clearly have political appeal as well: people benefiting from the first round of reform are more likely to support further instalments of the programme.

Clearly a simple and abrupt move to *laissez faire* is not a Pareto improvement if, as suggested above, it leads either to widespread falls in real wages or, where wages are supported, to widespread unemployment. Moreover many of the responses to these are, in fact, likely to make the unemployment even more widespread – a minimum wage for example. The same is also liable to be true of unemployment compensation which raises the reservation wage and, if the budgetary position is not to deteriorate, requires raising taxes that reduce employers' ability to pay given wages.

What kind of intervention might render liberalization of trade and prices more nearly Paretian?

Consider an extreme case in which both a minimum wage and unemployment compensation are in place and continuous budget balance is required. Then it is quite possible that the introduction of a temporary or transitional general employment subsidy will make things better in a large number of ways.[3]

If the minimum wage is defined in real (inflation-adjusted) net (after tax) terms, and if labour is homogeneous and wages so flexible that, at least at unemployment rates in the teens, all labour is paid the minimum wage, then a low general employment subsidy will not raise the take-home pay of the previously employed. But it does reduce the cost of employing them, or others, at the minimum wage, so that more are employed and the subsidy paid on their account is smaller than the dole they previously received. Thus the net tax burden on previous profits, which are enlarged by the effect of the subsidy, actually falls, while output rises more than the newly employed workers' consumption so that the resources available for investment, whether at home or abroad, are increased.

Provided only that the subsidy is believed to be temporary, investment allocation is not distorted – all investment goes into the sectors with a long-term future. In this case the belief that measures that prolong the life of dying enterprises must stunt the growth of new ones is clearly false. Nor is such a subsidy inimical to privatization – quite the contrary. Governments have shown a sensible reluctance to close value-adding but loss-making enterprises which they dare not subsidize openly and cannot sell. If a general, non-selective (albeit temporary) subsidy made such enterprises' cash flow positive for a while, they could be sold and subjected to the financial discipline of the market.

Why is such a panacea nowhere in place? First perhaps due to a failure of analysis and nerve, but also because the conditions assumed in the simple model do not pertain in practice. Wages are sustained as much by convention as by decree, and labour is not homogeneous or mobile enough to force wages down to the reservation wage of the unemployed. Politicians do not have the credibility to commit themselves to phase out a subsidy.

Many of these objections would be met by a temporary structure of border taxes, so designed that when trade was liberalized freed prices did not move much from those previously in effect. Such a device would generate revenue; and it would tend to sustain employment while facilitating privatization and financial discipline, which might itself suffice to squeeze about 10 per cent of workers out of their previous jobs. (At any level of unemployment below about 10 per cent it is hard to justify interference in the market. If recent Western European experience is a guide, 10 per cent unemployment is liable to be the norm.)

The credibility of the temporary nature of the relief remains an issue but one of the merits of border taxes is that they can be used to borrow credibility from others. Many reforming economies are so small that border taxes would carry a significant trade-distorting cost. If several such economies had suffered similar distortions in the past, they would need similar temporary border taxes now, and if their reform processes were roughly synchronized they could benefit from a common set of border taxes whose temporary nature could be enshrined in an international treaty. Similarly, obligations to phase out the taxes could be entered into with the IMF, the GATT or the EC.

You may feel that I have stretched the meaning of the word ethics to the limit by discussing in the last two sections general matters of economic policy. I do not apologise, for one of my main themes is that many issues like inflation and, perhaps more clearly, unemployment, that certainly have moral as well as social significance, are not issues of personal but of political morality for voters, legislators, ministers and their advisers.

Mafia capitalism

This is less true of the issues raised by the rough and tumble way in which market economics and private property are being introduced into Eastern Europe – especially the successor states to the former Soviet Union. In using the term 'Mafia capitalism' in my title I do not mean to imply a high degree of organization or any Sicilian links. The people pointed out to me in Moscow as 'Mafia' were typically gypsy urchins. The term is thus loosely – but it is also widely – used.

I want to comment on three phenomena or propositions associated with Mafia capitalism – and note in passing that the upright leader of economic reform in Czechoslovakia has said that Mafia capitalism is better than no capitalism. It is sometimes argued that sufficient liberalization eliminates the scope for corruption and other 'Mafia' activities. This is, at best, a half-truth. Secondly, officials sometimes say that under capitalism one sells ones resources, talents or, in their case, permits, to the highest bidder. What some call corruption is merely the consistent application of market principles – this, too, is at best only half true, as there is a continuum of prices, corrective taxes, penal taxes, fines and bribes. Thirdly, corruption may be a reflection of *nomenklatura* capitalism – the exploitation of contacts and positions inherited from the old regime – rather than of Mafia gangsterism. How do they compare?

1.   The view that corruption and related activity is only possible in a regulated economy it at best a half-truth for two reasons. The first is that it exaggerates the extent of feasible deregulation. Quite apart from the fact that all OECD member states have employment, safety, land use, building and drug regulations, even the 'night watchman' state has to raise taxes, enforce the law and employ soldiers and policemen as the night watchmen themselves. Each and every one of these functions is capable of abuse and, indeed, has been more or less openly abused in the history of Great Britain – where judges used to become very rich (I am going back two or three hundred years) and army commissions used to be sold openly, officially and as a matter of policy as recently as 150 years ago. Oxford and Cambridge still sell MAs to people like me who qualify more conventionally only for a BA.

Thus while deregulation may reduce the scope for corruption it certainly will not eliminate it.

One of the forms of police corruption involving either their participation or, in many cases their passive connivance, is protection racketeering. There are some industries, such as construction and catering, where this is endemic in parts of the West, but there is also a systematic link to economies in transition. Racketeers are no more inclined to kill geese that lay golden eggs than are farmers' wives. Such geese are rare in stable market economies because, given time, competition erodes abnormal profit or (quasi-) rents. Reforming economies started some distance from market equilibrium and have had little time for their little competition to erode the quasi-rents associated with this initial disequilibrium. These quasi-rents are both the inducement and the means by which resources build up in the more profitable sectors and bid down the price of the goods in relatively short supply under the new conditions.

That is their positive role – they also act as a lure for racketeers and rent-seekers and, to the extent that they succeed in effectively taxing expanding sectors, the shift in resources is slowed and the life of the premium geese is actually prolonged to the disadvantage of the generality of egg-eaters.

Tax fraud is also quite possible in the unregulated transitional economies, especially if their inherited values make the scale of redistribution relatively high. Indeed, non-compliance with tax arrangements is a major problem, having only recently been a virtue in the face of a despicable regime.

2.   The problem raised by those who argue that permits should be sold to the highest bidder is a real one. If only a limited number of houses is to be built, should we not ensure that the licence is obtained by the person who values it most highly? Are not tradable pollution licences and milk quotas now in vogue in the USA and EC for just this reason? On the other hand, trade in votes and ration books tends to be frowned upon. There is a highly technical literature on the relative merits of tradable and non-tradable rations which parallels that on the merits of benefits in cash and kind.

Thus while it may be possible, it is not easy to rebut the claim that where they exist licences should be sold. What is easier to rebut is the claim that the proceeds should accrue to the issuing officer rather than to the Treasury – especially if the effect is to lead to more licences being issued than the authorities intended. The monopoly profit-maximizing supply is unlikely to be optimal. The monopoly does of course depend on only one office being authorized to issue licences, and if that right is valuable the office itself might go to the highest bidder as with the tax farming arrangements of the *ancien regime* that preceded the French Revolution.

3.   A less crude form of corruption involves trading permits and jobs, not for cash but for influence and for friendship. In most transition economies many officials of the old regime – the so-called *nomenklatura* – have retained positions of some influence in public administration and in enterprises. In some cases the enterprises are still state-owned; in others the *nomenklatura* have used their inside position to acquire *de facto*, or even *de jure*, property rights in the firm or its assets, especially during the period of confusion in the immediate aftermath of the collapse of communism.

In many cases these people were more competent and ambitious than ideologically tainted. Nevertheless they are not popular, and that they should be the principal beneficiaries of privatization does not consolidate political support for reform.

The new regime is further discredited if these same people, and their friends in the administration, thrive on mutual favours.

Thus both the crude corruption of Mafia capitalism and the slightly more subtle corruption of *nomenklatura* capitalism are social evils reflecting unethical, indeed criminal, behaviour which should be as rigorously prosecuted as honest resources admit.

A more general conclusion that I draw from this section of my discussion is that in the journey from a very heavily to a moderately regulated state (such as that typical of OECD members), the formerly centrally planned economies should probably plan to move temporarily further in the direction of deregulation than may be their long-run goal.

The reason for this is that the human and moral capital required for the institutions to run even a moderate regulatory regime is not readily available, and particularly is not likely to be found among the officials and ambience of existing institutions with related functions. While there may be some merit in converting KGB men into tax collectors, officials of the old state trading organizations should probably not be appointed as customs officers.

The regulation of a market economy requires regulators who can work comfortably 'with the grain' of the market. Old central planners and former branch ministries are not the right people or institutions for the job. For this reason a relatively fresh start is called for. Also, a lighter level of regulation should make it easier to find the resources to suppress residual corruption so that the new institutions face more compliant actors. A (probably untypical) example here is that the smaller government can be made in the interim period, the further taxes can be reduced – which should make it easier to establish better habits of compliance than those established when non-payment of taxes to a despised regime was almost a moral duty, and better habits which might survive a raising of rates under a stable democracy in a growing economy.

Finale

I am aware that the moral philosophy has been swamped by the economics in this chapter – as, if the newspapers are to be believed, is true of much else in life. Nevertheless I hope that the economics was of some interest and that some people are convinced that even if the relief of poverty, unemployment (and inflation) are matters of political rather than personal morality that does not mean that personal morality is confined to the home (let alone the bedroom). On the contrary not only does it have a place in the even greater privacy of the polling booth, but a successful market economy depends on trust, respect for property, compliance with the law and the payment of taxes – not to mention restraint from gangsterism!

Notes

1.   This is the argument of Chapter 19 of Keynes's *General Theory* (1936).
2.   See Flemming (1987).
3.   See Flemming (1993).

References

Flemming, J.S. (1987), 'Wage Flexibility and Employment Stability', *Oxford Economic Papers*, **39**, 161–74.

Flemming, J.S. (1993), 'Unemployment and Economies in Transition', in Bos, D. (ed.), *Public Policy and Economic Organisation*, Vol. 3 of Economics in a Changing World (proceedings of the Tenth World Congress of the International Economics Association), Basingstoke: Macmillan.

Keynes, J.M. (1936), *The General Theory of Employment, Interest and Money*, London: Macmillan.

5   What moral constraints for business?
Norman Barry

Introduction

Despite the collapse of communism, the disintegration of many socialist ideals, and the spread of market capitalism throughout much of the world, a question mark still hangs over the morality of business enterprise (De George, 1982; Beauchamp and Bowie, 1992). The system as a whole may be respected, occasionally approving reference is made to the contribution it makes to human freedom, but doubts are persistently raised as to the ethical validity of the means which are typically used to bring about its success, and reproaches are frequently expressed about the end which it is commonly conceded to be about – mere utility. The success of capitalism seems to be tainted by the fact that it is powered by self-interest. Moral action has traditionally been associated with self-sacrifice or altruism. No doubt this claim underlies the conventional Christian objections to free enterprise and the profit motive. Profit is commonly, if mistakenly, thought to be only possible because of the exploitation of the ignorance and vulnerability of others. Even if these moral strictures are answerable, commercial activity, whatever its utilitarian advantages, has never been ranked very highly on the list of human achievements by the philosophers, from Aristotle to the present. Even the fact that from the 18th century onwards the rise of commerce has been associated with peace, in contrast with previous eras in which the pursuit of glory through war was highly valued, has been insufficient to assuage the critics.

No doubt the rash of business scandals that has occurred during the last few years has fuelled the animosity towards capitalism. The fact that these have mainly been straightforward crimes, which involve no technical ethical problems at all, has made little difference, except perhaps to add credence to the conception that business appeals to people with dubious moral motives. That is why much of business ethics seems to be concerned with a kind of therapy: how can businessmen be made to behave morally? Again, in conventional business ethics, the difference between immorality in business and crime has become blurred. That exploitation of opportunity, which is essential to business success, is not often distinguished from gross immoral behaviour, and that in turn has become criminalized. Actions which involve no discernible harm to others have now become crimes when in the past they had been deserving only of moral censure; the infamous Blue Arrow trial may be an example of this. The deliberate blurring of the technical violations by Michael Milken with the blatant wrongdoing

57

of Ivan Boesky may be another. The former's greatest sin was to earn a lot of money. Indeed, because of the unequal rewards that it makes possible, capitalism does not gel with prevailing egalitarian moral sentiments.

In such circumstances it is not surprising that a book written nearly 300 years ago should have such contemporary resonance. I refer to Bernard Mandeville's notorious *Fable of the Bees* (1705). In this he made his famous distinction between virtue and commerce. In the fable, the bees in their virtuous state are discontented and impoverished but when they are 'immoral', beneficence results. He claims that 'the grand principle that makes us social creatures, the solid basis, the life and support of all trade and employment, without exception is evil' (Mandeville, 1924, p. 236). Hence, the 'private vices', greed, selfishness and so on, turn out to be public virtues since they drive the economic system. The Wall Street of the 1980s may be a contemporary example of this phenomenon: the takeover battles and greed-driven corporate raids offended popular morality but they could be said to have brought about necessary corporate restructuring (Barry, 1991, Chs 4 and 5). Even debt had its virtues since it turned out to be an admirable way of disciplining corporate managements (Jensen and Meckling, 1976, pp. 349–51).

Adam Smith, of course, restored morality to commerce by stressing that the values of probity, honesty and justice, which actually characterize the business relationship, turn traders into genuine moral agents (despite some familiar criticisms he made of the merchant class). Yet Smith was eager to demonstrate the social value of self-interest with his famous observation that it is this which motivates 'the butcher, the baker and the brewer' to provide us with our dinner, not their benevolence. What Mandeville particularly had as his target was that more expansive view of morality that goes beyond the enforcement of conventional rules and which demands that we suppress our private desires in order to advance a supposed public good. His comments have relevance to those contemporary business ethicists who talk of the social responsibility of the corporation, a duty that extends beyond obedience to law and conventional morality to the positive promotion of social goals, at the possible cost to its shareholders.

There is more than a faint echo of Mandeville in Milton Friedman's famous recommendation to corporate executives; he said that their 'responsibility is to conduct the business in accordance with their desires, which generally will be to make as much money as possible, while conforming to the basic rules of society, both those embodied in law and those embodied in ethical custom' (Friedman, 1992, p. 57). In going beyond this, and engaging in socially valued activity, for example, enforcing possibly inefficient 'fair' employment practices, taking account of local interests and present employment in plant relocation, and engaging in charity, executives are betraying the interests of the stockholders and disrupting the 'principal–agent relationship' which is at the basis of the modern corporation.

There is, however, a kind of morality behind this non-moral, or at least ethically neutral, behaviour. It is utilitarianism. The movement of the 'invisible hand' will be cramped and constricted once business agents are distracted from their goal of pursuing profit. This is perhaps not quite fair to Friedman (1962, Ch. 1), since the maximization of individual liberty (which includes economic liberty) is his primary goal; but the main thrust of his argument for the market is its wealth-enhancing features. The familiar problems of 'market failure' and public goods can be, with some difficulty, incorporated into this framework. If not everybody gains from this process, at least more gain through it than from any other known economic system. The imposition of social duties on business via the actions of executives is in fact socially harmful; in Friedman's argument it is also immoral since it deprives owners of their rights.

It is clear that there are constraints on business within Friedman's system, although they are primarily of a minimalist, even negative, kind. Whether one calls them deontological, that is deriving from the theory that certain rules are intrinsically binding irrespective of any increase in well-being that their observance may produce, or 'maxims of prudence' which businessmen ought to follow in order to advance their long-term interests, is immaterial. In either case they impose limits on the opportunities for immediate advantage which an unrestrained market might permit. The market and the law (especially) do eventually catch out immoral behaviour but they are relatively slow, and their tardiness does allow for breaches of conventional morality to go unpunished. It is for this reason that business has adopted codes of restraint, largely to forestall costly regulation. But even this limited morality is difficult in business. Such co-operative behaviour undoubtedly involves 'prisoner's dilemma' problems, and although these have been shown to be surmountable in many social fields, because business is a sphere in which self-interest predominates, such co-operation is less likely to be forthcoming here than elsewhere. The fact that, in the West especially, it is conducted at 'arm's length' and in circumstances of relative anonymity means that pressure to conform to rules is likely to be less effective than in more intimate social arrangements. These problems are especially important with regard to the environment where the perpetrator of the wrong is often not identifiable: pollution itself is not unconscionably harmful, it is the additional polluter that generates the problem. Furthermore, the victims of pollution are widely dispersed and difficult to organize. Still, it seems to me that it is only through obedience to rules of self-restraint that we can make sense of the oft-quoted expression, 'ethics in business pays'. Mandeville would no doubt have insisted, with wry amusement, that this self-restraint, if it exists, is not a virtue at all but a more complex affirmation of the egoistic motivation. But it does nevertheless involve the exercise of some discipline – which might be thought impossible by a Mandevillian psychology.

However, the tendency of American business ethics has been to extend the range of constraints on business beyond the prevention of harm and the observance of minimalist standards (Freeman and Gilbert, 1988). The corporation, for example, is regarded not as an engine of prosperity with an ownership structure and a contractual form designed to maximize profit, but as a privileged legal arrangement whose rationale can only be validated if it acts virtuously in society. This approach openly challenges the notions of profit and individualism that undergird capitalism. To the extent that such social activity almost always harms shareholders (their consent would not be required) it cannot be plausibly maintained that ethics pays. Indeed, some American ethicists produce the *reductio ad absurdum* of deontological business ethics by arguing that business is only acting morally when it incurs loss in the pursuit of some specific moral end. The virtuous businessman can only be the one who pursues 'social justice' while everybody else free rides on his morality (Bowie, 1991).

The market
Business operates in competitive markets and it is noticeable that in the last two decades, while disquiet has increased at the alleged immorality of business, approval for markets has steadily increased. Socialists, alert to the distaste for vast collective enterprises operating independently of anything except cumbersome, and potentially corrupt, political control, have been eager to embrace the benefits of decentralized exchange. They have even invented something called 'market socialism' (Miller, 1989). Whether or not this expression is oxymoronic, it is certainly true that those who use it wish to detach the market mechanism as far as possible from business or capitalism.

It is easy to see why. The free market is an essential mechanism for co-ordinating the necessarily dispersed information that exists in society, and the price mechanism provides those signals by which individuals can be non-coercively directed towards benefiting themselves and others. The decentralized exchange system is the means by which creativity in human beings can develop, new possibilities for improvement can be exploited more or less painlessly and individual autonomy achieved. Whatever utilitarian value the market has is supplemented by the moral bedrock on which it rests: voluntarism. This must be a key concept in anybody's ethical vocabulary. I do not mean to deny that many problems remain, for example, externalities, public goods and inequality of access, but only to suggest that no order would be moral (let alone efficient) which eliminated the market.

The problems of business ethics are generated not by the concept of the market but by the way that it works, and the fact that certain institutions and practices spontaneously produced by it may be the cause of those phenomena criticized by moralists. What I am referring to here is the difference between the market order as described in the textbooks and the real world of markets which businessmen inhabit:[1] the difference between perfect competition and market process (Kirzner, 1973).

Leaving aside the moral significance of motivation (self-interest) it is surprising to notice just how close the ideal of perfect competition is to some fairly conventional, and non-controversial, ethical precepts. This was not, of course, the intention of the original authors of the model, they were simply laying down scientifically the conditions for the achievement of an efficient allocation of resources. But what they said has, accidentally, ethical significance.

Briefly, in the perfect competition model, all agents are fully informed of present and future circumstances, prices clear all markets, entry is costless, earnings reflect exactly the contribution to productivity made by factors and there are no externalities. What is noticeable here is the absence of at least two phenomena which are central to business: profit and the firm (for convenience I shall treat the firm and the corporation as equivalents). Profit arises only when there is error and where there exists inequality of information to be exploited. Under perfect competition nobody can be cheated or used as a mere means to the ends of another (in the sense described by Kant) precisely because each agent will know all that is relevant to any possible transaction. In theory, there is considerable equality alongside maximum efficiency since factor earnings will reflect marginal productivity. Inequality of initial resource endowments remains, however. But this is not relevant to the scientific theory. I would not have thought it was relevant to business agents in the real world either. It is a problem that properly belongs to government.

There will, in this model, be no firms or corporations, that is, the joining together of agents to achieve collective purposes (under quasi-authoritarian power structures), because instantaneous transacting between atomized individuals means that there are no permanent institutions that could inhibit individual freedom. As we shall see, many of the problems familiar to business ethics arise primarily from the existence of corporations, with their apparent legal privileges and the power that they allegedly exercise in society.

I am not suggesting that the conditions of perfect competition can be transformed into an ethical recipe for modern business ethics. It is by definition exclusively individualistic and therefore says nothing about communal obligations that may be relevant to commerce; it is silent on moral rules of trust and reciprocity (the 'Golden Rules', if you like) that are necessary for the business relationship, and its uncritical acceptance of self-interest is offensive to modern moralists. Nevertheless, an understanding of it does partially explain how ethical problems arise and how they may be resolved. One obvious example is the securities market in real-world economies, where information is at a premium and it is inevitably asymmetric. Profit here is entirely a product of one agent's alertness to the use to which his knowledge can be put. Is this 'fair'? This problem clearly could not arise under perfect competition. I do not suggest that business ethicists make any use of the distinction between perfect competition and market process (they seldom show much interest in the meaning of market behaviour), but it seems to me to be the only way to make sense of their criticisms of modern capitalism.

Of course, in the perfect competition model there is, as Frank Knight rightly asserted, no competition. There is nothing to compete for, no profits, no experimentation in various forms of economic organization and no efficiency improvements to be made. If one can meaningfully speak of ethical constraints they are automatically provided by the system. The justification for real-world markets, characterized as they are by ignorance and uncertainty, is presumably that they show a tendency towards efficiency. The price system constantly signals information to the participants about profitable opportunities, and freedom under the law provides facilities for innovation in industrial organization. However, success in this process invariably generates inequalities which often look unjustifiable; dependent as they often are on the exploitation of ignorance. To what extent does the presence of ignorance undermine the voluntariness and mutual advantage that is normally thought to characterize exchange?

Profit, payment above marginal productivity, inevitably emerges in imperfect markets but it has always aroused hostility because, superficially, it seems not to be necessary to draw the factors of production into their most productive uses. It depends entirely on one person's alertness to gaps in the market. To some people its pursuit is a sign of the market's fecundity in creating new value; entrepreneurial profit is not only of utilitarian benefit, it is also that to which the entrepreneur is entitled because he is the originator of such value (Kirzner, 1989). To others it is simply a form of exploitation, or just luck. The fact that it seems to compromise the mutual advantage that occurs through exchange is no doubt the reason why Christian writers on economics identified the morality of the market with the long-run equilibrium price. But would there be any creativity if this were to be considered as a legitimate constraint on business behaviour?

Furthermore, complex problems of 'rights' emerge in real markets as well as intense controversy over property. To refer to the securities market again: does justice here require a level 'playing field', in which each participant is equally informed? Or does it merely insist on the absence of fraud and deception? Is the 'insider dealer' to be permitted to use his special knowledge on the stock market or is he merely a thief who has stolen company property (knowledge)? Are outside shareholders treated unfairly? Overall there is the question of whether positive, that is statute law, (which may be efficiency-reducing) should be used to create justice in the market for information, or whether this can be left to private contracts, enforceable at common law, between company owners (stockholders) and employees. Still, it is clear that the establishment of a perfect, level playing field in securities really would turn the stock market into a game of chance.

The original insider dealing case in America, the Texas Gulf Sulphur saga (1968), provides a fascinating example of 'level playing field' theory. Employees of the company had made a valuable mineral strike and delayed disclosure until they had bought stock. They were eventually successfully charged with insider dealing, though it was not clear that they knew they were acting illegally. Indeed, the legal ruling looked retrospective. Interestingly, no one suggested that they were under any obligation to reveal to landowners in the area the news of the mineral strike. They sold their land at low prices in complete ignorance. There was no level playing field for them. Were they unfairly treated?

The irony is, then, that the process towards the perfection of markets may often involve offence to conventional moral values. That creativity in market relationships may often be interpreted as a simple example of exploitation of ignorance and may also involve harm in that the innovation produced may upset legitimate expectations. A corporate raider might create genuine economic value, his alertness to the fact that the share price of a company understates the potential value of the assets can be seen as a genuine act of creativity and a much-needed threat to slothful managements. But the effect of his skills may be devastating to local communities and established workforces. A notion of acceptable self-interest, as described by Adam Smith, may quickly degenerate into sheer greed when the raider is not interested in the reorganization of corporate assets but purely in the break-up value of companies that might actually be viable. The market may well be the mechanism for the correction of error; but it is in the nature of the process that we can never be sure that every step in it contributes to overall co-ordination. To many observers of the 1980s, there was no difference between legitimate error correction and pure avarice.

It might very well be argued that the raider is at least advancing the interests of the shareholder, who may have no other sanction against entrenched man-agements except to sell his stock, but against this a more expansive view of business ethics would advance the interests of stakeholders, who might be any person or group (employees, suppliers and local communities) likely to be adversely affected by market processes. This is overtly to bring communitar-ian notions to bear on the market: the latter is no longer to be reduced to transactions between individuals and corporate 'persons' with well-defined property rights, but is to include claims that may not derive from any sort of ownership. No doubt the ethical minimalist would argue that all of this simply reduces efficiency and the creativity that freedom produces. The difficulty here is that whereas economists see the overall benefits that market processes generate for purely abstract, non-identifiable agents, the business ethicist tends to particularize, that is, he concentrates on the directly observable adverse effects of these relentless processes. Of course, evidence of these is normally easily available. That is why the constraints under which business ought to be conducted are much more stringent for moralists than for economists.

Corporate moral wrongs

However, even under the minimalist view of business ethics the fact that markets are never perfect presents problems. The pursuit of profit may be acceptable, but what limitations should be placed on the means? There are some well-discussed examples of business wrongdoing which do not involve the kind of strong, that is positive, welfare-enhancing, constraints mentioned above.

One thinks immediately of the Ford Motor Corporations's manufacture, in the late 1970s, of the Pinto car (De George, 1992, pp. 130–37): it knew this to be an unsafe vehicle. The rear-mounted petrol tank exploded in collisions, which resulted in the deaths of some people. The issue did not simply involve Ford's manufacture of an unsafe vehicle; there is no such thing as a perfectly safe product and the attempt to produce one would price most goods out of the reach of ordinary consumers. The real immorality of Ford's action arose out of the exploitation of ignorance. Engaged in fierce competition with General Motors to produce a cheap small car, they were advised by their engineers that the costs in rectifying the fault would put them well behind in the race. However, they calculated the likely costs in civil damages, were an accident to occur and, since these were less than the rectification costs, they went ahead as planned, with disastrous results. One doubts that action would have been any less reprehensible even if they had warned potential customers of the danger, but the problem necessarily arose out of ignorance.

Presumably, even Friedman's reference to the constraints imposed by 'customary morals' would be sufficient to condemn Ford's action, but in many other cases it is not at all clear what these constraints imply. The difficulty is compounded by the anonymity of the market – it weakens moral constraints on the pursuit of profit. The producers of unsafe goods do not know the potential victims.

A similar, and only slightly less controversial example, was Nestlé's sale of 'infant formula' to Third World mothers (Barry, 1991, Ch. 2). This was a highly useful product, especially to these customers, but it required careful use (it should not be mixed with contaminated water). Ignorant mothers used it incorrectly and some deaths resulted. What was worse, the company continued to market the product after the health dangers were well publicized. However, the example is not straightforward. It is plausible (just) to mount a defence of Nestlé from a straightforward utilitarian perspective; this is indeed what the corporation did in the face of organized protests and boycotts. The company argued that the social benefits outweighed the costs. Furthermore, Nestlé could not be held responsible for the misuse of their product as there was no deception in its marketing and advertising. Were they not treating the consumers as autonomous agents capable of making rational choices? However, certainly a broadened utilitarianism would have taken account of the possible harmful effects on a minority in its use of the formula. It would be a morally crass form of cost-benefit analysis that permitted the gains (however massive) of the majority to override completely the harms caused to a minority (however small). Furthermore, it would certainly not be inconsistent with utilitarianism to take account of the informational disparities between various sets of consumers.

It would therefore be possible to regard Nestlé's action as condemnable from that version of arm's length morality which is primarily utilitarian in emphasis. However, the major criticism of Nestlé was grounded in a much more controversial deontological framework. The corporation was actually accused of violating the rights of mothers in the Third World by continuing to market the product in the face of mounting unfavourable evidence. Apparently the competitive impulse and the desire for profit had been decisive over all other considerations. The consumers had been used only as a means to the end of corporate commercial success. This seems a much more contentious case; for there was nothing in Nestlé's actions that specifically violated the rights of individuals and, indeed, a genuine deontological ethic would not turn upon the material interests of individuals (as perceived by outsiders) but upon a recognition of their personal autonomy. It is rather odd to describe restraints, either voluntary ones exercised by the corporation or compulsory regulation by the state, as rights-enhancing, since a market transaction which leaves the consumer to make up his own mind is an expression of individual choice and autonomy.

It is true that normal business practice (rather than high-flown moral philosophy) is sufficient to guide companies in such cases, and in the long run such action often pays off. In the famous Tylenol case, packets of the medication had been poisoned by someone and then planted in a very small number of shops (Nash, 1990, pp. 38–43). Though the company, Johnson & Johnson, was in no way responsible for this (and there was only a slight danger) it immediately withdrew all of the product, incurring a considerable loss. As it turned out, it earned moral plaudits for this action and eventually regained market share. Cynics have suggested that there was no real moral merit in what Johnson & Johnson did; that it was actually good marketing strategy. Still, when the action was taken the company was not to know that it would be successful; it was taking a risk since there was no real evidence that there would have been a drop in public confidence if it had not withdrawn the product.

It would perhaps be more appropriate to describe such actions as prudential rather than moral. Indeed, when writers maintain that 'ethics pays' that is presumably what is meant. The same phenomenon is at work when businesses formulate the aforementioned codes of conduct to restrain them when there are considerable information gaps between consumers and producers. They are designed to curb immediate acts of gratification which, if generalized, would be harmful for everybody. They are presumably not meant to turn all moral action into altruism. What is so difficult about business is the enforcement of these general rules against free riders. Ethics in law and medicine are easier to maintain because of the monopolistic nature of these professions. Still, no doubt Friedman would say that business codes were anti-competitive.

Corporate social responsibility

However, contemporary American business ethics has gone beyond the concern about the wrongs committed by corporations, wrongs which could be avoided while still maintaining profitability. The emphasis now is on the positive social duties which corporations are under a duty to perform, even at a loss in returns to shareholders and wages to employees. In ordinary morality they might very well be called supererogatory duties, that is desirable in themselves but not compelling. But business, apparently, is in a special position; morality decrees that it is not merely to refrain from harm but to act for the general good. Furthermore, this injunction is not delivered to shareholders alone, which would make more sense, but to managements.

The ethical theory here marks a decisive shift in the nature of ownership. As one writer puts it, '... the reason for paying returns to owners is not that they "own" the firm, but that their support is necessary for its survival' (Evan and Freeman, 1992, p. 82). Apparently it is perfectly acceptable to use owners merely as means to the ends of others. This attenuated form of ownership severely constrains what firms can do. Profit-maximization according to many business ethicists is only legitimate if it takes its place alongside the pursuit of contentious social goals, for example, vigorous affirmative action policies, care for the environment beyond that required by positive law and property rights, implementation of welfare schemes and support for the local area in which the firm is situated. There would appear to be a notion of Kantian duty at work here, that is certain actions are obligatory irrespective of self-interest or the effect that they might have on the operation of the 'invisible hand'. It is noticeable that these injunctions are addressed primarily to the managements of enterprises; they are to be constrained in the way that they handle a company's assets (these are resources which are no longer truly individually owned). This is somewhat different from owners acting charitably. Even Mandeville could not object to this (though he would no doubt think it absurd).

The rationale for this activity, however, could be derived from an explanation of the emergence of the firm. It is a kind of non-market phenomenon that develops because of the transaction costs involved if individuals were to negotiate with each other to perform every task (Coase, 1937). The pooling of resources and the assumption of risk creates corporate entities that superficially belie the neoclassical model of economic co-ordination. The contract of employment is loose and bilateral and it commits the worker to anything demanded of him by the employer. Although he is free to leave, business ethicists still maintain that his liberty is compromised by the existence of the corporate power structure. As one writer, not unfriendly to the phenomenon, famously put it, corporations are 'islands of conscious power in an ocean of unconscious co-operation' (Robertson and Dennison, 1960, p. 73).

Of course, my description is somewhat crude. There are many types of contractual arrangement within firms, indeed genuine entrepreneurship can and does exist within the organization. Also, the authoritarian structure I have briefly described conceals the fecundity of the market in generating a range of economic forms, not many of which are freedom-reducing in any significant sense. However, it seems to be the model used by business ethicists and appears, superficially, to be an admirable case for 'moralization'. The fact that it has emerged spontaneously does not mitigate its coercive features in the eyes of business ethicists. The separation of ownership from control has provided another reason for imposing constraints on what corporations may do.

Anyway, a large part of the critique of corporations, and the rationale for their moral reconstruction, derives from the claim that their features are a result of specific state and legal action; they have not developed spontaneously at all, it is argued. The corporation does appear to have certain legal 'privileges', for example limited liability, legal personhood and a kind of permanent existence. It is an artificial person that has many of the attributes of a biological person. Indeed, some American business ethicists say that it has enough of them to be liable for criminal prosecution (it can have a *mens rea*). I shall consider this problem in the final section of this chapter.

Of course, free marketeers deny that any of these things constitute legal privileges; the corporation, they say, cannot do anything which is not permitted to the individual. What look like corporate advantages are simply the result of freely negotiated individual agreements which the state merely recognizes. After all, nobody is compelled to deal with organizations that protect themselves through limited liability. There is a whole range of commercial arrangements, from simple partnerships through to multinational corporations. Still, business ethicists maintain that the corporation could not exist without the positive law of the state and that there is a kind of 'social contract' between it and society (Keeley, 1988). In return for its legal privileges the corporation must fulfil certain social duties and avoid excessive use of its acquired powers (the common law and the market are not considered to be adequate checking mechanisms).

There are many valid criticisms of this view. One is an obvious market-derived objection. A competitive market provides benefits to anonymous agents. The more duties that are imposed on it, the more costly its activities become, and this results in disbenefit to the same anonymous agents. Because of their anonymity they are less likely to attract the sympathy of business ethicists. In fact, only in conditions approaching monopoly would there be sufficient 'slack' to permit much corporate social activity (and I presume monopoly would be objected to on other grounds). In fact, a more feasible business ethics would concentrate on making markets more competitive, attacking collusion between business and government and between commercial agents themselves (something which Adam Smith famously criticized).

There is obviously a conflict between the demands of the conventional market system, that the first duty of management is to maximize shareholder value, and the injunction from business ethics that the corporation should serve some collective purpose. If market processes are allowed to work they will reflect and solve this conflict. Thus, if shareholders do not object to social activity then they will accept the consequent loss. However, one can safely predict that most will demur, so that a company that pursues non-commercial ends will be highly vulnerable to a takeover. In theory, then, the pursuit of non-pecuniary goals is limited by the transaction costs involved in takeovers. Of course, the proponents of an activist business ethics are also opposed to the takeover mechanism itself, so that the restrictions on this that have occurred, for example in the USA, at state and federal level, can be seen as part of a wider policy package. Or perhaps they can be interpreted in terms of 'unintended consequences', as part of a development whereby voluntary business ethics becomes legislated business ethics; where one intervention unwittingly spawns a whole string of interventions.

The argument, however, does direct our attention once again to the question of who is to be responsible for this supererogatory ethical action – the management or the shareholders? As is well known, corporate executives are not averse to it. It is, after all, not primarily their money that is at risk. Surely, at this level, ethical conduct should involve a choice between profit and principle. Presumably, corporate executives get some utility from ethical action of this type (as well as an easier life). But there is ample evidence of ethical investment; funds which are directed towards moral companies (they tend to be concerned with 'green' issues) and the avoidance of corporations that trade with unacceptable political regimes. No free marketeer could object to this. Indeed, there are good examples of shareholder activism diverting a company to more ethically desirable goals. However, there is obviously a difficulty here for fund managers, who possibly face a conflict between their duties towards the fund members (who in most cases will not be rich but simply future pensioners) and a commitment to a moral principle. However, I think that the conflict is more likely to be regarded as a genuine one where basic moral principles with regard to what is right conduct are involved, rather than in areas which encompass the supererogatory duties. This distinction is rarely made in business ethics.

Stakeholder theory

At the heart of business ethics and the theory of corporate responsibility is the distinction between the stockholder and the stakeholder. Since the firm is not to be seen primarily as a profit-maximizing enterprise, according to the theory it must take account of all who have an interest (including employees, suppliers and local communities) in it, whether or not they are owners. This underlies the argument that stakeholders should have representation on boards of directors; in some business ethics circles it is even said that they should have a decisive voice on topics such as plant relocation, lay-offs and community relations. There is some institutional reflection of this in the representation of trade unions on the supervisory boards of German companies (though the owners' voice is decisive on key issues).

If stakeholder theory is to make any sense it must assume that there exists an hierarchy of values which can order the various claims that impinge on a company; otherwise corporate policy will be the result of trade-offs and compromises between competing groups: a kind of microcosm of what happens in national politics. In one sense, the market orders competing claims, but this is meaningful only in the context of a property rights regime. However, according to business ethics, the claims of property are only to be considered as equal (if not inferior) to other demands, not superior to them. It is true that most business ethicists have recognized this problem (two writers[2] have even invoked the notion of a fully informed 'metaphysical director' who will make Solomon-like decisions in such conflicts); but it is likely to be insoluble in pluralist societies, where capitalism tends to develop, and where there is disagreement about ends.

There is also the problem of the range and extent of stakeholder interests. In complex economies, which integrate many different agents, everyone to some extent depends on everybody else, even though formally they are at arm's length. If a business decides not to relocate (even though efficiency dictates that it should) because that would cause unemployment in an area in which it has been long-established, is it not harming the interests of those who would have been employed in the new area? Why are they not to be regarded as stakeholders in a progressive economy? Only in a non-pluralistic society, where there is a determinate set of ordered values, could such decisions be rationally made outside the market.

It is true that some notion of the stakeholder could be incorporated into a more realistic business ethics. For example, an enterprise that has dealt with a particular supplier for a long period of time, and built up harmonious relationships, may be advised not to abandon him/her just because an alternative has appeared at a cheaper price. Grasping shareholders may simply be wrong, and their desire for short-term profit may bring long-term harm. It is perfectly feasible that the establishment of long-term relationships may be good for business (this, it is claimed, is what happens in Japan and Germany). But it has little to do with business ethics, although there may be some moral reason for maintaining more 'intimate' commercial relationships despite the risks involved. It is better interpreted as an example of prudence. The market itself will make the final decision as to which enterprise has been the most prudential.

There is a real sense in which stakeholder theory is very far from being moral, and may be quite inconsistent with the social responsibility thesis. To protect the interests of particular groups, and to exempt them from the possibly adverse consequences of normal market processes, is to be selective in one's morality. It hardly looks to be consistent with the principle of justice which, at the very least, demands fair treatment of individuals, unless good moral grounds can be produced for differential treatment. Is the mere fact of an established position within a corporation a good ground? Of course, if shareholders were responsible for distributing the largesse, or taking extra-market actions, one could not complain. But if managements, as is normally the case, take such decisions in their role as moral agents, one should expect them to take a wider view. If they are to be genuinely 'socially responsible' they should not privilege their own stakeholders.

Henry Manne (1972, p. 29) quotes the instructive example of Coca Cola's attempt to provide a kind of private enterprise welfare system for its employees who were working in rather poor conditions in Florida (they were immigrants who had made the calculation that however bad their conditions were while working for Coca Cola they were at least better than the alternatives facing them in their home countries). The result of Coca Cola's benevolence was, of course, an increase in its costs and therefore a reduction in employment opportunities. Yet all the moral attention was focused on the welfare scheme, and none of it on those unknown people who had been made unemployed by it. This is a classic example of the visibility of corporate ethics and the invisibility of its unintended consequences.

It is difficult to provide a case for the managements of corporations engaging in a positive social role without provoking conflicts of interests, either with their shareholders or with other groups in society. This is not to say that the 'invisible hand' always works beneficently. It may not; not only in the familiar areas of externalities and public goods, but also in the fact that it creates victims through its remorseless reallocative process. Entrepreneurship produces, in Schumpeter's telling phrase, 'gales of creative destruction'. However, to expect corporations to bear the full responsibility for the effects of the operation of impersonal forces would be to blur moral responsibility and most likely would coagulate the processes of adjustment to change. This could produce even worse results, in a utilitarian sense, than allowing corporations to perform their conventional role. Welfare, outside the market, is primarily a government responsibility and for business to assume it is not only a kind of conceit but also a usurpation of the political role.

Nevertheless, it is still plausibly maintained that people are harmed by certain corporate actions and these are condemnable by even a minimalist ethics. The takeover mechanism is an obvious example, since people's customary expectations are upset by the apparently greed-driven (Mandevillian) motivations of financiers. It is not clear that it is necessitated by efficiency considerations; evidence is mixed as to whether it does lead to an increase in shareholder value (Peacock and Bannock, 1991). It is doubted whether shareholders in the acquiring company gain much, if anything. Certainly, some highly successful economies, Japan and Germany are the obvious examples, seem to do very well without it. Corporate raiders are presumably not particularly moral agents (few people would value their right to freedom, though the judgement of the majority could be mistaken), and if it turned out that their actions were economically unnecessary, then what justification remains for them?

However, before seizing on this as yet another example of market failure, one or two cautionary notes should be made. Different societies generate different business cultures and it would be unwise to assume that business practices can be transplanted anywhere under the rubric of a supposedly universal ethic. Co-ordination in the aggressive arm's length style of business in the USA is undoubtedly different from that in the more intimate and co-operative style in Japan, but that is not to say that it is necessarily worse.[3] The rather contemptuous way in which shareholders are treated by Japanese corporations would be quite unacceptable in the USA. Moreover, in Germany ordinary shareholders (as opposed to the banks) are showing resentment at their exclusion from any managerial role in the corporation.

These questions are as much, if not more so, economic than moral, and perhaps we will have to wait for an (unpredictable) economic history for the answers. However, there is a moral question which is relevant to the ethics of takeovers. How could a rule be devised which distinguished ordinary, efficiency-enhancing industrial reorganization from takeovers driven by pure greed? In economies like the USA and the UK, where the mechanism may be the only method of disciplining managements, there will always be the temptation for 'bust-ups' to take place which may have little economic value. But since the human mind can never have the knowledge necessary to make discriminations between competing claims to economic value, it is difficult to imagine state interventions improving on the market. These are quite likely to generate worse results, both ethically and in terms of rationality, than those produced by an admittedly imperfect market. The attempt to design rules in this area may well fall victim to the rationalist's delusion of seeking perfection in an inevitably flawed world. It is also likely to disintegrate into a series of *ad hoc* interventions, with all the damage to the rule of law which they entail. It is almost certainly the case that interventions in the spontaneous process of market correction in otherwise open and anonymous systems will be inspired by politics rather than rationality.

Corporate crime

The moral and legal constraints that have been imposed on business behaviour have been added to recently by the development of the theory of corporate criminal responsibility. Given that corporations do sometimes act wrongly there is the ethical question: who exactly is responsible for corporate misbehaviour? The corporation is a legal personality liable for torts and any other civil wrongs committed in the course of its operations. There is nothing controversial in the arrangement whereby individuals, through pooling their resources in order to pursue commercial gain, make themselves liable in civil law for the possible costs that might be incurred in business. The fact that the owners (as the principal) and possibly the Board of Directors (the agent) ultimately bear the costs of civil action is neither inconducive to efficiency nor offensive to morality. The separation of ownership and control theoretically makes no difference; for the entrustment of corporate assets to managements necessarily involves risk. The joint-stock company emerged precisely for efficiency reasons; authority is delegated by owners to managers. Indeed, the possibility of civil action is an incentive for shareholders to take a more active interest in the affairs of companies that they formally own.

In theory, the rights and duties of the corporation derive from the rights and duties of individuals. In practice, however, the development of the modern corporation, and its alleged social and economic power and falsely proclaimed immunity from corrective competitive processes, has led to the demand for a greater control over its activities than that provided by civil law and the market. Hence the growth in the past few years of criminal prosecutions of corporations (for which managements take the 'blame' but shareholders pay the costs). Undoubtedly, the theory that corporations are the creatures of positive law, with its strong implication that the corporation is something more than a legal artifice constructed solely out of the legal rights of concrete individuals, has been influential. If this is so, then it would be possible to make a *prima facie* case for subjecting the corporation to duties that do not arise from the actions of individuals. A corporation could be treated as more than a legal artifice. It is perhaps a 'real' person of whom one could predicate actions independently of the actions of its individual members (for example, its board members and employees). Superficially, it sounds bizarre to speak of a corporation as an artifice capable of performing actions normally thought to be only possible of biological persons, but there is some philosophical literature on the subject of corporate personality (French, 1984). This has some relevance to the questions of whether it is legitimate to prosecute corporations for manslaughter, theft or any other serious criminal offence.

In neither law nor morality has the question of corporate criminal responsibility been solved, though the issue has been given a much more thorough airing by lawyers and philosophers in America than in Britain. The first important example of alleged corporate responsibility for serious crime was the prosecution of the Ford Motor Corporation (in the Pinto case) for reckless homicide in 1980 (Reidenbach and Robin, 1989, pp. 38–42). Of course, criminal responsibility had previously been attributed to corporations, both in Britain and the USA, but this had been for less serious (and less obviously personal) offences: normally those which lie on the borderline between torts and crimes. Although Ford's original defence to the charge of reckless homicide, that is a corporation is not a person and cannot commit homicide, was rejected, it was eventually acquitted at the trial. Nevertheless, there have been some successful prosecutions of corporations for criminal offences. Recently, fines and restitution totalling $5 million were imposed on the Boeing Corporation for a two-count felony of corporate theft. The Exxon Corporation was fined one billion dollars over the Alaskan oil spill (even though they had already paid the clean-up costs) because they had apparently breached an obscure criminal statute. The example of the unsuccessful prosecution (1990) of the P&O Company for corporate manslaughter over the deaths involved in the Zeebrugge tragedy is close to the American models. In English law it has been established that corporations can be charged with crimes which were once thought possible only of biological agents, but as yet the conditions for success are extraordinarily difficult to satisfy.

Irrespective of how the law develops, the question of corporate liability for serious crime raises fundamental ethical (not to mention philosophical) issues. Can the notions of intention and *mens rea* (a guilty mind) seriously be attributed to non-human agencies? Who are the people to be considered as representative of the corporation in such actions? What kind of penalty is appropriate if and when the offence has been proved? Should shareholders, who normally have nothing to do with criminal action (individuals who own corporations do not normally set them up in order to commit crimes!), have to pay the heavy fines that result from convictions? Is it likely that an increase in, and extension of, corporate liability will make it easier for culpable individuals to hide behind the 'corporate veil'? Finally, and of growing importance, does the criminal prosecution of the corporation reflect a desire for 'vengeance' in response to horrific accidents rather than a concern for justice?

The claim that corporations can act intentionally and have a guilty mind arises out of a proposed distinction between an 'aggregate' and a 'conglomerate' (French, 1984, Ch. 5). An aggregate is merely a set of individuals who may do things together which they could not do separately; but it does not constitute a permanent, ongoing entity capable of being identified independently of these discrete individuals. However, a conglomerate has the feature of permanence and it exists irrespective of the changing composition of its membership. It is identified not by the attitudes of particular individuals, but in its collective biography or record of its aims and purposes, successes and failures. American business ethicists tend to locate the separate identity of the corporation with the Corporate Internal Decision Structure or CIDS (which contains basically its fundamental telos, or state at which it aims). This identification enables us to say that the corporation can 'act' and hence exhibit intention and responsibility. Nevertheless all writers who take this position do say that it still requires some individual endeavour to activate the CIDS.

Now it is true that many organizations (and not only firms) have a life that transcends the lives of individual members, and we do often speak metaphorically of collective minds. It is also true that individuals can do things in concert, both good and bad, which they cannot do as individuals. The whole nature of the corporation presupposes that part of its essence is that it has a life beyond the lives of its individual members. The identity of corporations cannot simply be established by knowledge of the identities of its individual, and possibly transitory, members.

However, none or all of these features taken together is sufficient to justify the claim that corporations can act intentionally in the way that humans can, or that they can experience shame, regret, remorse and so on. In fact, philosophers systematically misunderstand the nature of the business enterprise. It is a means to an end, not an end in itself; a legal contrivance which individuals have discovered to advance their interests in a world of uncertainty. Indeed, its purpose in most important respects can only be established by reference to the purposes of those who manage and own it. Since, as I suggested earlier, the corporation only exists because of the absence of perfect competition, it must be understood primarily in economic terms. In a world of uncertainty the success of the corporation depends upon the skill and ingenuity of its individual members in exploiting profitable opportunities.

Only if corporations behaved in a regular and predictable manner, and every agent fulfilled a specified and unchanging function, could it be plausibly said that it displayed a group cohesiveness equivalent to biological personhood (and even then this description would be little more than a metaphor). But in fact a great deal of entrepreneurship goes on in corporations, and this is the phenomenon of identifiable individuals responding to changes in the environment and displaying that alertness to new opportunities in the inevitable flux of economic life. If these known individuals are to be rewarded for their contributions to the success of the enterprise then surely they are equally responsible for its moral (and other) failings. There is a compelling moral symmetry here. Sometimes it may be difficult to disentangle individual efforts in necessarily collaborative activities, but the exposure of a practical problem is not the same thing as demonstrating some metaphysical truth.

From this it follows that guilt for criminal wrongdoing should properly be attributed to the individuals directly concerned. Indeed, those business ethicists who insist on corporate liability also claim that both individuals and the corporation should be prosecuted for crimes. In fact, the issue was confused in the Ford Pinto case because none of the culpable executives was put in the dock. This has not happened since (in the Boeing case, a separate charge of theft was brought against the person who had actually committed the offence). It is the case in English law that the 'directing mind(s)' of the corporation have to be identified and convicted before a criminal charge against the company can succeed. Moreover, these individuals must be very closely connected with the criminal act itself.

The desire to go beyond individual actions in the kinds of horrific events that lead to corporate manslaughter charges is understandable. Civil actions, no matter how costly they may turn out to be, seem superficially inadequate an expression of the revulsion that people obviously feel at these, sometimes avoidable, distressing events. It is because criminal law has an 'expressive function', that is, it indicates strongly society's disapproval of certain actions, that the desire to 'punish' corporations should be so prevalent. Nevertheless, the imposition of punitive civil damages may well be a solution to this problem, although the generosity with which the courts in the USA award them creates other difficulties.

None of these observations justifies the claim that a corporation is a 'person' which exists, for moral purposes and for the punishment of the criminal law, apart from the actions of individuals. Of course, corporate executives may often find themselves in difficult positions, circumstances in which 'loyalty' to the company might compete with the constraints of ordinary commonsense morality, but such dilemmas are not solved by shifting responsibility to, or sharing it with, an artificial (if not quite 'fictitious') agency. Surely those Ford executives should have resigned and 'blown the whistle' on the company for the manu-facture of the Pinto. Indeed, evidence was readily available of the morally crude calculations that were made of the costs of civil actions if crashes were to occur compared to the production losses if the fault were to be corrected. These calculations were made by individuals.

Presumably, the logical implication of the argument that corporations can be liable for serious criminal offences is that boards of directors should be imprisoned, even if they were not immediately involved in the reckless or other behaviour that caused the catastrophe. This would be plausible if individual board members could be shown to be responsible by the normal processes of criminal law. But in the Zeebrugge case, for example, the catastrophe was caused by the irresponsible action (actually, inaction) of the bosun and his immediate supervisor who both failed to comply with company procedures (*The Times*, 20 October 1990). It may be the case that, in this and other similar tragedies, the procedures were inadequate. Again, is this not a problem of locating responsibility in particular officers, difficult though that may be? If the corporation is to be charged in addition to identifiable individual wrongdoers then the consequences can, logically, only be massive fines. These are ultimately paid by the owners (share-holders) who had nothing to do with the original offence.

It is also important to note that in the Zeebrugge case the judge specifically refused to allow the whole range of individual wrongs to be aggregated so as to constitute a corporate wrong. This of course makes the crime of corporate manslaughter extraordinarily difficult to prove in law. What is the point of bringing this type of charge against a corporation if it really is the case that only an individual can commit it?

The morality of corporate responsibility for crime is as confused and inde-terminate as is the law. Sometimes it consists of a certain kind of utilitarianism: that the threat of criminal sanctions is the only way of ensuring that the constant monitoring of activities, which is required for the avoidance of tragedies, actually takes place. It is assumed here that civil actions for damages, to which nobody could object, are inadequate. Yet utilitarian considerations could point in a different direction; it is plausible to suppose that corporate enterprise would be seriously deterred if the organization were criminally and collectively respon-sible for every wrongful action committed by subordinates. In advance of more convincing moral argument, it is tempting to assume that current pressure for the criminal prosecution of corporations for actions normally thought possible only of biological persons is motivated by 'vengeance' rather than by justice. It is an attitude no doubt strengthened by the low esteem in which the corpo-ration is held, especially in American society. Some such view was implied by the judge in the Exxon case. In rejecting the company's original plea bargain he said that the fine would not sufficiently affect its profitability. Thus he was not concerned simply with the wrong committed (which would be required by justice) but with raiding the 'deep pockets' of Exxon.

Despite the failure of the prosecution of the P&O Company in the Zeebrugge case (it could not be proved that its procedures constituted 'obvious' risk) the possibility of corporate liability for serious criminal action was accepted in principle and this runs counter to the principal–agent theory of the corporation. For while that theory can accommodate the idea that the principals (the owners) should shoulder the burdens of civil liability (indeed, it may encourage investors to be more active in the monitoring of the companies they own) it is difficult to see what kind of theory could convincingly establish the guilt of a collective institution which is required for cases involving criminal intent.

The argument that without the invocation of a corporate mind (embodied in the Board of Directors) crimes would go unpunished because of the difficulty of establishing individual responsibility is unpersuasive on two grounds. First, this practical difficulty is not, surely, the same thing as theoretically establish-ing the case for corporate criminal liability. If that were the argument then particular persons (board members taken collectively) would be 'used' as means to advance some particular end. The end (safety) itself is obviously good, but it is at least plausible to suggest that this could be advanced without the potentiality of rights-violation that the invocation of corporate criminal liability involves. Perhaps the judge in the Zeebrugge case had this in mind when he refused to allow individual wrongful acts to be 'aggregated' so as to produce a collective wrong. Also, he did not dismiss the case against the culpable individuals involved in the tragedy (although the prosecution did not proceed against them).

Secondly, I wonder how difficult it really is to establish individual responsibility? In most of the standard cases in the USA, and all of them in Britain, individuals are charged along with the company. Most theorists of corporate criminal liability admit that the actions of a corporate person have to be activated by biological persons. If this is so, then it is surely in principle possible to identify individual agents in human tragedies.

Conclusion

The attempts to create new categories of 'corporate' crime reflect a pattern that is common in business ethics: that is, the attribution of a special set of moral duties to business personnel and their related organizations. They are not to be bound merely by the normal rules of just conduct but are expected to perform social actions that are not demanded of other agents. No doubt the inspiration for this derives from the fact that the undesirable motive of self-interest is thought to be more prevalent in business than in other activities – though this can be doubted. The power that business is supposed to wield in society may also fuel demands for a greater moral accountability.

However, apart from the adverse effects on prosperity that this new moralism may have, it can be questioned whether business ethics constitutes a special type of enquiry. This is not to deny that business agents often act wrongly, or indeed that they often face acute moral dilemmas, but our traditional moral language is rich enough to describe such phenomena. Members of all professions, and individuals in their daily lives, face similar – if sometimes less dramatic – problems and responsibilities. Those that seem to occur uniquely in commerce might be better explained by a proper understanding of the competitive process and the legal environment in which it takes place, than by constructing a special business ethics. By contrast, the extended set of moral constraints for business that has emerged in recent years seems to have been constructed in some ignorance of the way competitive markets work, and in defiance of those property-rights structures and contractual relationships on which they necessarily rest.

Notes

1. This distinction derives from Austrian economics and was perfected in the economic thought of Ludwig von Mises (1966) and F.A. von Hayek (1948).
2. Evan and Freeman (1992, p. 83). Such a person would have to be perfectly impartial.

3. Those who think that the 'face to face' business relationships in Japan are more moral than in the West should reflect on the Nomura scandal in 1991. The brokerage house protected certain privileged clients from stock price falls.

References

Barry, N.P. (1991), *The Morality of Business Enterprise*, Aberdeen: Aberdeen University Press.

Beauchamp, T. and Bowie, N. (eds) (1992), *Ethical Theory and Business*, Englewood Cliffs, New Jersey: Prentice Hall.

Bowie, N. (1991), 'New Directions in Corporate Responsibility', *Business Management*, July–August.

Coase, R. (1937), 'The Nature of the Firm', *Economica*, **4**, 386–405.

De George, R. (1982), *Business Ethics*, New York: Macmillan.

De George, R. (1992), 'Ethical Responsibilities of Engineers in Large Organisations', in Beauchamp and Bowie (eds), *Ethical Theory and Business*, Englewood Cliffs, New Jersey: Prentice Hall.

Dettmer, J. (1990), 'Avoidable Human Errors Afloat and Ashore', in *The Times*, 20 October.

Evan, W. and Freeman, R. (1992), 'A Stakeholder Theory of the Modern Corporation: Kantian Capitalism', in Beauchamp and Bowie (eds), *Ethical Theory and Business*, Englewood Cliffs, New Jersey: Prentice Hall.

Freeman, R. and Gilbert, D. (1988), *Corporate Strategy and the Search for Ethics*, New Jersey: Prentice Hall.

French, P. (1984), *Corporations and Corporate Responsibility*, New York: Columbia University Press.

Friedman, M. (1962), *Capitalism and Freedom*, Chicago: Chicago University Press.

Friedman, M. (1992), 'The Social Responsibility of Business is to Increase its Profits', in Beauchamp and Bowie (eds), *Ethical Theory and Business*, Englewood Cliffs, New Jersey: Prentice Hall.

Hayek, F.A. von (1948), *Individualism and Economic Order*, London: Routledge and Kegan Paul.

Jensen, M. and Meckling, W. (1976), 'The Theory of the Firm', *Journal of Financial Economics*, **3**, 305–60.

Keeley, M. (1988), *A Social Contract Theory of Organisations*, Notre Dame: University of Notre Dame Press.

Kirzner, I. (1973), *Competition and Entrepreneurship*, Chicago: Chicago University Press.

Kirzner, I. (1989), *Discovery, Capitalism and Distributive Justice*, Oxford: Oxford University Press.

Mandeville, B. (1924), *The Fable of the Bees*, Oxford: Clarendon Press.

Manne, H. (1972), *The Modern Corporation and Social Responsibility*, Washington: American Enterprise Institute.

Miller, D. (1989), *Market, State and Community*, Oxford: Oxford University Press.

Mises, L. von (1966), *Human Action*, Chicago: Henry Regnery (first published in 1949).

Nash, L. (1990), *Good Intentions Aside*, Cambridge: Harvard Business School.

Peacock, A. and Bannock, G. (1991), *Corporate Takeovers and the Public Interest*, Aberdeen: Aberdeen University Press.

Reidenbach, R. and Robin, D. (1989), *Ethics and Profits*, New Jersey: Prentice Hall.

Robertson, D. and Dennison, S. (1960), *The Control of Industry*, Cambridge: Cambridge University Press.

6 Fairness in the rationing of health care
John Broome

Introduction

We used to be able to pretend to ourselves that a health service could give everyone all the health care they needed: rationing was not required. That was never so in truth, but by now even the pretence has become impossible. New medical technology can do wonderful things for people, but at such a cost that we cannot afford to use it for everyone who could benefit. Some people will have to be denied treatment that would do them good. Some people will die, and some people will suffer, not because we do not have methods of treating them, but because we cannot afford to use all the methods we have. So somehow it has to be determined who will be treated and who will not. This is rationing.

There is a crisis in the health care systems of many developed countries. These systems were set up with the aim of giving people the care they needed, not to deny care to some. Now that explicit rationing has become inevitable, they need to find a way of doing it. Some people think rationing could be avoided if only we cut out waste, or if only we spent more on the health service. No doubt there is waste in every health care system, and perhaps we do not spend as much on health as we should. Nevertheless, however much we streamlined the system, and however much we spent, there would always be ways we could save more lives and prevent more suffering. For instance, we could build on every street a resuscitation unit for the victims of heart attacks, and that would save some people's lives. If we do not think it worth the cost, we are denying those people treatment that would have saved them. That is rationing. Besides, money is not the only scarce resource in medicine. Organs for transplants are another. There are not enough donor organs for everyone who needs one, so they have to be rationed.

Rationing is inevitable, then. How should it be done? There are two questions here. One is what objective should our system of rationing aim at? What criteria should it apply in deciding between people who need treatment? The other question is, what institutions and procedures should we have to put these principles into effect? Is a market of some sort the best way of doing it? Should we put the rationing decisions into the hands of general practitioners or specialist administrators? And so on. I am going to concentrate principally on the first question: what objective should we be aiming at in distributing our scarce medical resources to the people who need them?

Doing the most good

The answer that springs immediately to mind is that we should try to use our scarce resources in a way that will do the most good. This seems obvious, and I think this answer is the one that seems right to many health economists. If resources can do more good used one way than another, then they should be used where they can do more good. This thought underlies the use of quality-adjusted life years (qalys) as units for measuring the value of different sorts of treatment.

Qalys are a measure of the good a treatment does: its benefit. Medicine can do two sorts of good. It can prolong people's lives, and it can make people's lives better while they last. Qalys combine these two sorts of benefit into a single measure. A year of healthy life counts as one qaly. Years in less good health are adjusted downwards by an adjustment factor that is meant to measure the quality of life. If you receive some treatment, its benefit is measured as the number of qalys you will have after the treatment less the number you would have had without it. If some treatment saves your life and gives you 15 more healthy years, the benefit of that treatment is 15 qalys. If the treatment leaves you in poor health, your quality of life will be rated lower. Your 15 years of life will be counted as, say, ten qalys. On the other hand, suppose you have a treatment that does not extend your life, but allows you to live your remaining years in good health rather than as an invalid. If you live for 20 more years, and your quality of life is very much improved, that might count as a gain of ten qalys.

Since qalys are supposed to be a measure of benefit, they can be used to help direct resources to where they will do the most good. We can compare the qalys a treatment produces with its costs. Economists have calculated the cost per qaly for different treatments. For instance, a kidney transplant may cost around £1 400 per qaly, and replacing a shoulder joint about £600.[1] So it seems that money spent on replacing shoulder joints does more good than money spent on a kidney transplant. Most authors who use qalys would draw the conclusion that we should direct our resources more towards shoulder replacements and less towards kidney transplants.

There are severe technical difficulties with the use of qalys. One is the difficulty of setting up the scale of quality adjustment factors for different states of health. If a state has an adjustment factor of a half, that means two years in this state will be judged equally as good as one year in good health. How do we decide what state of health merits this evaluation? This is a tricky question, which economists have argued about for a while. But I am going to set it aside in this chapter.

Instead, I am going to concentrate on the general idea that we should use our resources to do the most good. I said that qalys are intended to implement this idea because they are supposed to measure the benefit of a treatment. Is this really the right objective for using the medical resources we have available? At first it seems obviously right. But if the figures I have given are correct, it means rationing kidney transplants more severely than shoulder replacements, because they are more expensive per qaly. But kidney transplants save lives. Is it right to deny some people the chance of life in order to use the resources for improving the lives of other people? Perhaps that is not so obviously right. When we are considering alternative treatments for a single patient, no doubt it is right to choose the one that will be most beneficial to her. Qalys are often used for this purpose.[2] But they are also often used for distributing resources between patients.[3] And in this case other considerations besides benefit may come into play. For instance, we surely need to be concerned with the rights of patients as individuals, and with acting fairly between them. To some extent these considerations may conflict with maximizing benefit. I shall come back to this.

Rationing by the market

What alternative principles are there for rationing, besides aiming to do the most good? I am going to mention two. I shall not dwell on the first, but I can scarcely avoid mentioning it in the context of rationing. I mean the market. The market is not a criterion for rationing resources, but it is a method of rationing resources which leads to a particular distribution of resources between people. If we had a free market in health services, then particular people would end up with particular treatments that they or their insurers have paid for. Other people would be denied treatment because they could not afford it, being uninsured or possessing insurance that did not cover their needs. That is how resources would be rationed. The market would do the rationing for us, and we would not need rationing criteria.

The merit of a market as a rationing system is that, if it works properly as it is supposed to work in theory, it will be 'efficient'. This is the merit of a market that economists know well. (They also know that a market in health services is very unlikely to be efficient, because it will not work as the textbook theory supposes. There are many sources of 'market failure', which I do not need to go into here.) Being efficient means that a market avoids wasting resources in a sense. But it does not mean that the resources are necessarily used in the way that does the most good. This is the main point I want to put across about the market. Economists know this well, too, but some non-economists may have been deceived by the economist's notion of efficiency. When economists say a market is efficient, they mean that, if the market is running properly, there is no other way resources could be used that would make someone better off without making someone else worse off. You could not improve someone's lot without damaging someone else's. This is the sense in which the market avoids waste. But there is absolutely nothing in economic theory that suggests a market distributes resources in a way that does the most good. This is why I called the market an 'alternative' to the criterion of maximizing benefit.

It is obvious that an ordinary market in health services would not lead to the best use of resources: it would not ensure that the resources are used in the way that will do the most good. In a market, who gets treatment is determined by who can afford treatment, or who can afford good insurance, rather than by who will benefit most from treatment. Rich people will have treatments that do them little or no good, and poor people will not get treatments they desperately need. However, as we move towards a market in Britain, it is by no means an ordinary market we are moving to. It is generally called a quasi-market. Except in the fully private sector, who gets treatment is not determined by what the patients can afford, but by what their districts or fundholders can afford. In principle, if funds were properly allocated among the fundholders, this system could be manipulated to achieve the greatest possible benefit. Funds would have to be allocated to the places where they were most beneficial. But nothing like this will happen automatically. We have no reason to expect that the market will lead to the best use of resources.

Organ transplants and urgency

That was an aside. My chief purpose is to look at a different criterion that comes into play when distributing medical resources among people, besides the criterion of doing the most good. I mean the criterion of fairness. I shall introduce it with two examples.

My first example is the selection of patients to receive a liver transplant. There is a shortage of livers, so some people who need a new liver cannot be given one. Consequently, they will die. Somehow, it has to be decided who will receive a liver, and who will die instead; somehow, livers have to be rationed. What criteria should be used? One criterion that actually is used in the UK and North Italy (the two places I know about) is the urgency of the case. In the UK a patient's position is defined as urgent when the patient will die within three days if she does not receive a transplant. Urgent cases are given priority over less urgent cases. The same happens in North Italy. In both countries, this criterion has been arrived at by consultation among the transplant teams involved.[4]

Now, if the aim was to use the available livers to do the most good, urgency would play no part in allocating them. Each liver would be used where the chances of a successful transplant were highest. It would go to the patient who has the best chance of success with it, and that means the patient whose tissue matches it most closely and who is in good condition for the operation. There is no reason why transplants into patients with the most urgent cases should be the most successful. So giving these patients priority means to some extent overruling the criteria of tissue matching and good medical condition. It means that, in the long run, the supply of livers will not be used in the way that will do the most good.

So why use the urgency criterion? This is not the only case where we give priority to people in immediate danger of death. When people are trapped in a mine, or under the sea, we are willing to spend a great deal of money to rescue them. If the same money was used in other ways, it could save more lives. For instance, in the long run money will save more lives if it is spent on making mines safer rather than on very expensive rescue operations. But we are much more reluctant to abandon a few people to certain death than we are to expose many people to a risk of death, even if the result is that we save fewer people in the end. This is one way in which we fail to use our resources to maximize the benefit we derive from them. Why? Have we a good reason, or is it merely sentimentality on our part?[5]

One good reason is a concern for fairness. If a patient with an urgent need misses a liver as it becomes available, that is her last chance gone. If someone with a less urgent case misses a liver, she may get one later. So by giving priority to urgent cases, we are doing something to equalize people's chances of survival. We are increasing equality in this respect, and that means we are treating the patients in urgent need more fairly. Given the scarcity of livers, the distribution of them is effectively a lottery. By giving priority to the urgent cases, we are helping to make it a more equal lottery in which people have more equal chances.[6] This promotes fairness.

This, then, is one example where fairness operates as a criterion for the distribution of resources in medicine that conflicts with the objective of doing the most good. If we wished only to do the most good we would ignore the urgency criterion, but fairness requires us to take it into account.

The Oregon Plan and discrimination

Another example comes from the reception of the Oregon Plan in the USA.[7] The Oregon Plan is perhaps the most comprehensive attempt there has been to develop an explicit system for rationing medical resources. Initially at least, it is intended to apply only to recipients of Medicaid. The purpose of Medicaid is to provide medical services for people who cannot afford private insurance. But in Oregon, as in other states, many of the poorest citizens are not eligible for Medicaid, so that they receive no medical services at all. Even so, Oregon, like other states, finds its spending on Medicaid is very large and growing fast. The reason is that, once a person is eligible for Medicaid, she is entitled to receive any treatment her doctor believes would benefit her, however expensive it may be. So a great deal of money is going to those who are lucky enough to be eligible (chiefly mothers and children), and none to those who are not.

Oregon's plan is to extend Medicaid to everyone whose income is below the official poverty line, but to ration all these people to a particular range of treatments. The state drew up a list of 709 'condition–treatment pairs', each specifying a particular treatment for a particular illness. It ranked them all in order from the one it considered most beneficial to the one it considered least beneficial. Then it decided that Medicaid would pay for the top 587 items in the list, and none beyond that point. The criteria it used for ranking the condition–treatment pairs are obscure in detail. For instance, it did not use the cost per qaly, as one might expect if it was trying to derive the maximum benefit from its resources. Nevertheless, it is clear that it was principally aiming at the benefit the patient derives from the treatment. Benefit as measured by qalys was the major element in the assessment process.

Medicaid is partly financed by US federal funds, so the Oregon Plan could not be implemented without agreement from Washington. The Plan has been accepted by the Clintons, but it was originally vetoed by the Bush Administration on interesting and unexpected grounds. It was said to discriminate against disabled people, which is forbidden by federal law. It was said to discriminate because it counts the life of a disabled person as less valuable than the life of a person in good health.

It is certainly true that the Oregon Plan counts a disabled life as less valuable than a healthy life. Suppose you and I are about the same age, and each of us has a fatal disease. Our diseases are different, but each can be treated. Your treatment would save your life, and restore you to good health. My treatment would save my life, but leave me disabled. Your treatment would rank higher in Oregon's list than mine, and it could happen that you might receive treatment and I might not. This is because the healthy life you would live after treatment is counted as more valuable than the disabled life I would live. This is inherent in the whole idea of adjusting the value of a life for its quality. It is inherent in the use of qalys.

Now, the fact is that life in good health *is* generally better than life with a disability. If there is a choice, for a single patient, between a treatment that saves her life and restores her to good health and one that saves her life but leaves her disabled, the former is the right choice. It is right because it gives the person a better life. If, next, the choice is between saving your life and restoring you to good health, and saving my life and leaving me disabled, it still seems that the former is the right choice to make. It certainly does more good, and I do not think that choosing it can possibly be said to discriminate on grounds of disability. At present, before our treatment, neither you nor I is any more disabled than the other, so discrimination is surely impossible. Nevertheless, the danger of discrimination really does lurk in the use of qalys. Suppose you and I have the same disease, but I am disabled anyway. Saving your life will restore you to good health; saving mine will restore me to my previous disabled state. Treating you would score higher on a quality of life scale than treating me. If this was used as a reason for treating you and not me, that would indeed be discrimination. I would be denied the treatment simply because I am disabled. So far as I can tell, the Oregon Plan does not in fact discriminate in this way.

It ranks only condition–treatment pairs, irrespective of who has the condition. It is not concerned with the circumstances of individuals, and it takes no notice of individual disabilities. Even so, it would be discriminatory if disabled people were particularly susceptible to certain conditions, and if those conditions were ranked low for that reason. But I do not think that happened in the Oregon Plan. I think the White House was wrong to make its accusation. So far as I know, no one who uses qalys has fallen into the trap of discriminating in this way.

Fairness
Still, all that saved the Oregon Plan from the trap is that it did not apply qalys at the individual level. If qalys were consistently applied to deciding who gets treatment and who does not, they would discriminate against disabled people, because they count the continuing life of a disabled person as less valuable than the continuing life of a healthy person. This does not mean they are failing in their purpose. Their purpose is to pick out the treatments that do the most good. And extending the life of an average healthy person does more good than extending the life of an average disabled person, since an average healthy person's life is better than an average disabled person's. What it means is that doing the most good is not the right thing to be aiming at in deciding between a healthy person and a disabled one. It would be wrong to discriminate against a disabled person on the grounds that her life is less good. It would be unfair. Doing the most good would lead to discrimination, which is a sort of unfairness.

Once again, fairness is in conflict with the aim of doing the most good. Oddly enough, this fact is implicitly recognized in the use of qalys themselves. Up to now, I have said that qalys are aimed at doing the most good. But actually that is not so; they are implicitly adjusted in the direction of fairness. They count a year of healthy life for one person the same as a year of healthy life for another. But actually, some healthy people lead much better lives than others. For instance, some healthy people live in miserable poverty, and others live in comfortable and pleasant sufficiency. A year lived in comfort is undoubtedly better than a year lived in poverty, yet they will be counted the same by qaly measures. Saving the life of a poor person will be valued equally with saving the life of a rich person. No doubt they should be valued equally; it is a merit of qalys that they do so.[8] It would be wrong for the health service to discriminate against a person just because she is poor and therefore not enjoying a very good life. If we wanted to do the most good, we would discriminate. But for fairness, that should not be our aim, and qalys recognize this.

So qalys go this far in avoiding discrimination, but not far enough. The quality adjustment embodied in qalys is for states of health only. Consequently, qalys ignore a person's wealth because wealth is not a state of health; they do not discriminate on grounds of wealth. On the other hand, a disability is a state of health, so qalys would discriminate on grounds of disability if they were consistently applied.

Fairness versus doing the most good

The two examples I have given show that there is another objective that rationing should aim at besides doing the most good. It should also aim to be fair. The two aims conflict to some extent. So we are faced with the problem of reconciling them or balancing them against each other. How should this be done?

One possibility is to adjust the objective of doing the most good in the direction of fairness. Instead of trying to maximize the total benefit to people, we would maximize a different total, appropriately adjusted. I have already said that qalys do this to some extent. Instead of aiming to maximize total benefit, they aim to maximize a total that excludes discrimination on particular grounds.

This approach can certainly accommodate some of the requirements of fairness, but not all. The fundamental problem is that fairness is not really about maximizing anything. It is about equalizing, not maximizing. It requires people to be treated equally.

To see the difference, notice there is a difference between valuing people's lives equally and valuing equality in people's lives. Valuing people's lives equally means counting a year of one person's life equally with a year of another's, even if one of the people is disabled, say. It is a matter of non-discrimination, and it is consistent with maximizing. It requires that we give equal weight to different people in what we maximize. So non-discrimination, which is one aspect of fairness, is consistent with maximizing. We need only maximize a non-discriminatory total. But valuing equality in people's lives is more demanding. It asks that people should actually lead lives that are equally long or equally good or equal in some other respect. In fact this is impossibly demanding; life is so uncertain that we cannot possibly expect equality in lives. Fairness cannot demand as much. But fairness does sometimes demand a sort of surrogate. It cannot demand that people should have equal lives, but when organs are rationed among the people who need them, it demands that as far as possible everyone should have an equal *chance* of living.

This is what I meant when I said that fairness is a matter of equalizing rather than maximizing. In this case it requires equal chances; in other cases equality in other things. This cannot be fitted within a maximizing objective. It means that balancing fairness against doing the most good will be a difficult task. It will certainly require serious work in theoretical ethics.[9]

Notes
1. These figures are from Gudex (1990).
2. For instance, Pliskin, Shepard and Weinstein (1980).
3. See Gudex, *op. cit.*

4.   My information about the UK was kindly given to me by Dr Peter Klouda of UK Transplant Services. For North Italy, see Nord Italia Transplant (1993).
5.   There is an excellent discussion of this question in Fried (1969). Fried finds only one possible good reason for this practice. I am adding a second.
6.   I have examined the fairness of equalizing chances in Broome (1990).
7.   The Oregon Plan is described and debated in Strosberg *et al.* (1992).
8.   As Culyer (1990) correctly says.
9.   I have tried to start this work in Broome (1990).

References

Broome, J. (1990), 'Fairness', *Proceedings of the Aristotelian Society*, **90**, 87–102.

Culyer, A.J. (1990), 'Commodities, Characteristics of Commodities, Characteristics of People, Utilities and the Value of Life', in Baldwin, S., Godfrey, C. and Propper, C. (eds), *Quality of Life: Perspectives and Policies*, London: Routledge.

Fried, C. (1969), 'The Value of Life', *Harvard Law Review*, **82**, 1415–37.

Gudex, C. (1990), 'The Qualy: How Can It Be Used?', in Baldwin, S., Godfrey, C. and Propper, C. (eds), *Quality of Life: Perspectives and Policies*, London: Routledge.

Nord Italia Transplant (1993), *Prelievo e Trapiento di Organi: Resconti 1992*.

Pliskin, J.S., Shepard, D.S. and Weinstein, M.C. (1980), 'Utility Functions for Life Years and Health Status', *Operations Research*, **28**, 206–24.

Strosberg, M.A., Wiener, J.M. and Baker, R. with Fein, A. (eds) (1992), *Rationing America's Medical Care: The Oregon Plan and Beyond*, Washington D.C.: The Brookings Institution.

7 The role of ethics in Keynes's economics
Robert Skidelsky

Introduction

Economists are starting to be interested once more in the place of ethical considerations in economics. This follows a widespread feeling that the economics of Margaret Thatcher and Ronald Reagan exalted greed at the expense of virtue; or, to put it another way, individual self-interest at the expense of community. Consideration of the role of ethics in economics has also been stimulated by the problems of development, the environment and the 'transition' of planned to market economies.

Economists' reliance on models of rational optimizing behaviour means that ethical criticism of economic processes and outcomes has tended to come from 'outside' economics, often from churchmen. Recently, there have been rigorous attempts by economists to demonstrate that morality 'pays' – that is, is rational behaviour from the individual's point of view.

It may be instructive to contrast these approaches with Keynes's attempt to ground economics in ethics. Whereas contemporary discussion is concerned with moral behaviour, Keynes was interested in the ethics of ends – with the question of what goods were intrinsically valuable. This interest testifies to an optimism in the power of human reason to penetrate to 'truth' which has now largely vanished.

In arguing that rationality was a property of ends as well as means, Keynes drew chiefly on the *Principia Ethica* of G.E. Moore, which influenced him profoundly when it was first published in 1903. Moore's 'ideal utilitarianism', which rejected the 'naturalistic fallacy' of defining good in terms of a natural object such as pleasure, set Keynes a problem about the relationship between wealth and goodness. This is largely absent from hedonistic utilitarianism, but is an important preoccupation in both Keynes's published and unpublished writings.

Keynes had much more trouble with Moore's account of the rationality of behaviour, and largely wrote his *Treatise on Probability* to correct what he thought was Moore's excessive emphasis on following generally accepted rules. His further concepts of 'weight of argument' and 'least risk' provide philosophically based rationales for his well-known preference for short-termism and risk aversion in both individual and public behaviour. I will conclude by considering Keynes's view of the role of justice in the proper ordering of economic relationships.

Bloomsbury economics?

'A man is not likely to be a good economist who is nothing else' wrote J.S. Mill. To be a good economist one must be good at other things too. It is the nature of these 'other things' and their relationship to his economics which I want to explore in Keynes's case. I want to argue that for Keynes economics was a branch of applied ethics; and to consider what effect his ethical beliefs had on his economic theory and policy advice.

Writing to William Temple, Archbishop of Canterbury, on 3 December 1941, Keynes explained that most 18th century writers on economics were churchmen.[1] 'Marshall always used to insist that it was through ethics that he arrived at political economy and I would claim myself in this, as in no other respect, to be a pupil of his'.[2] Such a claim might seem paradoxical from someone who declared himself to be an 'immoralist'.[3] Keynes's gift for iconoclastic utterance has been grist to the mill of anti-Keynesians. His most famous remark, 'In the long run we are all dead' was interpreted by Schumpeter (1952) as a 'childless' – he might have added godless – perspective. Childless becomes homosexual in Rees-Mogg's (1983) suggestion that Keynes's rejection of moral rules led him to reject the 'gold standard which provided an automatic control of monetary inflation'.

This view of Keynes's economics as the product of the closet rather than the cloister is, I believe, profoundly false. It rests on the superficial association of Bloomsbury with levity and immorality, and ignores the fact that the Bloomsbury disciplines of G.E. Moore, while adopting modes of expression designed to shock their Victorian elders, subscribed to, and tried to live their lives by, the ethical principles set out in the Moore's *Principia Ethica.*

How you respond to this value-system, or set about explaining its influence on Keynes's economics, is another matter. My one biographical comment is that the older Keynes got, the more anxious he became to preserve civilization's 'precarious crust' from its socialist as well as its *laissez-faire* wreckers. Chapter 12 of the *General Theory* is an ethical as well as technical polemic against stock market speculation. The relationship between an investor and his share should be like that between husband and wife, Keynes wrote; and in his own investment policy he started to practise the philosophy of 'faithfulness'. The best results possible in an uncertain world are achieved when people behave morally. These conclusions came to Keynes late. He was not a great believer in moral codes earlier in life, having too great a belief in the power of human reason. Indeed, his theory of probability, as will become clear, was conceived as an alternative to the need for moral codes.

The ethical impulse behind Keynes's economics is not to be found in the usual places. He was much less concerned with how a society's production ought to be organized and its income and wealth distributed – the classic domain of normative economics – than with judgements about what ought to be produced and what the level of production and employment ought to be – topics on which the classical tradition of his day was silent. His ethics are to be found in his macroeconomics, not his microeconomics. He saw the Depression as giving government the chance and duty to influence not just the level of demand, but the composition of demand.

Intellectual contexts: J.N. Keynes and Lionel Robbins

Keynes frequently called economics a 'moral science'. To understand what he meant let me recall two contemporary discussions of economic method, the first by Keynes's father, the second by Lionel Robbins.

J. N. Keynes's *Scope and Method of Political Economy* was published in 1891. Its main purpose was to settle the methodological 'war of opinion' between the Germans and Anglo-Saxons by a Marshallian compromise. Thus he identified the ethical school of economists with the Germans who held that there can be no purely positive science of economics. The ethical school, wrote J.N. Keynes:

> regards political economy as having a high ethical task, and as concerned with the most important problems of human life. The science is not merely to classify the motives that prompt economic activity; it must also weigh and compare their moral merit. It must determine a standard of the right production and distribution of wealth, such that the demands of justice and morality may be satisfied. It must set forth an ideal of economic development, having in view the intellectual and moral, as well as the merely material, life; and it must discuss the ways and means – such as the strengthening of right motives, and the spread of sound customs and habits in industrial life, as well as the direct intervention of the State – by which that ideal is to be sought after (J.N. Keynes, 1891, p. 23).

J.N. Keynes rejected the extreme claim of the ethical school that statements of 'is' and 'ought' were indistinguishable. The intrusion of ethics into economics will simply multiply and perpetuate sources of disagreement; if economics is to make progress as a science it must shed 'all extrinsive or premature sources of controversy'; its principles must be established 'independently of ethical and practical considerations'; 'political economy, regarded as a positive science, may, therefore, be said, to be independent of ethics'.[4] On the other hand 'applied economics' must embrace ethics, 'for no solution of a practical problem, relating to human conduct, can be regarded as complete, until its ethical aspects have been considered'.[5] These large concessions to ethics reflect the late Victorian attempt to moralize economic life.

In J.N. Keynes's account the line of division between positive and normative runs between theory and practice. His son turned this upside down. He denied that economic theory could be a positive science: value-judgements invaded all its propositions. As he wrote, famously, to Roy Harrod in 1938:

It is as though the fall of the apple to the ground depended on the apple's motives, on whether it is worth while falling to the ground, and whether the ground wanted the apple to fall, and on mistaken calculations on the part of the apple as to how far it was from the centre of the earth.[6]

On the other hand, unlike his father, he believed that 'normative' economics – the study of how people should behave – *was* objective in the sense that ethical ends could be rationally known. The data of experience – the subject matter of so-called positive economics – were constantly shifting; ethical truths were timeless. Nothing that Keynes says about methodology makes sense unless one keeps this framework in mind.

Maynard Keynes accepted his father's definition of economics as the study of man as a wealth-creator.[7] This provided a clear point of entry for ethical judgement. The peaceful pursuit of wealth could be morally (rationally) distinguished from the warlike pursuit of glory – a theme dear to the ears of Victorian political economists. Alternatively one could denounce the concentration on producing material goods as immoral. All 19th century parties to the debate assumed that rationality in behaviour had to be decided by reference to ethics, though not to ethics alone.

In his *Essay on the Nature and Significance of Economic Science*, published in 1932, just over 50 years after J.N. Keynes's *Scope and Method*, Lionel Robbins offered another definition of its subject matter which broke the link between the rational and the ethical. 'Economics', he wrote, 'is the science which studies human behaviour as a relationship between ends and scarce means which have alternative uses'.[8] The entire subject matter of economics is the study of utility-maximization under constraint. It follows that economics is not concerned with ends as such.[9] 'It takes the ends as given in scales of relative valuation and enquires what consequences follow in regard to certain aspects of behaviour'.[10]

The economist *qua* economist has nothing to say on the rationality of ends. 'Now in so far as the idea of rational action involves the idea of *ethically appropriate* action ... it may be said at once ... that no such assumption enters into economic analysis ... economic analysis is *wertfrei* ...';[11] and '... there are no economic ends. There are only economical and uneconomical ways of achieving given ends'.[12] Ethics cannot be associated with economics except contingently.[13] Moral issues are 'outside interests' for economists.[14]

J.M. Keynes's one brief reference to Robbins's work is dismissive. 'As against Robbins,' he wrote to Harrod, 'economics is a moral science and not a natural science. That is to say, it employs introspection and judgments of value'.[15] This is in the context of a diatribe against Tinbergen's econometrics, and must be read as a protest against the claim of economics to establish empirical knowledge of human behaviour. Nor would Keynes ever have defined economics as the study of economizing behaviour alone. The point of Robbins's strategy was to deflect criticism from economics by placing at its core rationality rather than greed. However, the point about the logic of greed was precisely that one could ask whether it was rational, whereas a critic of economics as defined by Robbins was reduced to questioning the ethics of rationality – a much weaker ground of attack.

Robbins was the first economist writing under the influence of logical positivism. The ends of life fall outside the scope of rational discussion; rationality attaches wholly to the means. Keynes believed that ends can be rationally known. Robbins's view may be seen as a secularized version of Lutheran or Jansenist theology: the ends of life are revealed by faith, not by reason, so reason attaches only to means. Keynes's view that the ends of life can be rationally known harks back to Plato, Aristotle and the Thomists.

Keynes's ethical framework

The ethical frame within which Keynes thought about economic problems was provided by G.E. Moore. Moore provided him with his ethical criterion for judging ends. However, in thinking about the duties of the state in relation to both ethics and economics, Keynes was greatly influenced by Burke, on whose political doctrines he wrote a long essay while still an undergraduate.

For Moore, the primary ethical question is 'what is good?' or 'what sorts of things ought to exist for their own sake?'. The question 'what ought I to do?' can be answered only by reference to the primary question, and to the probable consequences of action. Moore's doctrine is startling and austere:

> By far the most valuable things we know or can imagine are certain states of consciousness which may be roughly described as the pleasure of human intercourse and the enjoyment of beautiful objects ... It is only for the sake of these things – in order that as much of them as possible may at some time exist – that one can be justified in performing any public or private duty; ... it is they ... that form the rational ultimate end of human action and the sole criterion of social progress.[16]

The following comments are in order:

1. Moore's list of intrinsically valuable goods is very short. Keynes added knowledge to this list. The most ethically valued goods for Keynes are states of consciousness described by the phrases 'being in love', 'experiencing aesthetic emotion', and 'knowing the truth'. The connection between ethics and truth must be noted.
2. These ethical goods are not to be construed as statements of personal preference. Good was an objective indefinable quality of things, intuitively *known* to be present or absent. Rational people know what is good. Rationality, that is, attaches to ends, not just to means.

3. Moore's ethical doctrine may be described as 'ideal', as distinguished from hedonistic, utilitarianism, because that which is to be maximized is not happiness but goodness. The economist is enjoined to ask: what wealth-producing activities tend to increase or retard the production of the greatest possible goodness? The link between wealth and goodness is far more problematic than for Bentham. A sensationalist psychology combined with the great-happiness principle yields the straightforward conclusion that any desired increase in the aggregate of creature comforts is ethically desirable. This is not so in Moore's system. The connection is indirect, and always has to be argued.

4. In place of Bentham's 'felicific calculus' Moore offers the 'principle of organic unity' as a way not of measuring but of judging the quantity of goodness in a state of affairs. The chief use of the principle was to limit the power to sum goodness by reference to isolated states of consciousness on their own. Thus good states of mind are 'complex organic unities', the ethical value of which could be more or less than the sum of its parts. Keynes proposed that only states of mind are 'good', but that the goodness of states of mind could be improved or diminished by the 'fitness' of states of affairs. The doctrine of organic unity may be seen as a bridge between Moore's ethical goods and other moral aims. Will a state of justice improve the goodness of states of consciousness? How far is a life of action consistent with good states of mind? And so on.

5. Moore's utilitarianism shares with Bentham's the characteristic of treating instrumentally all values not specified as being intrinsically good. Liberty and justice are not 'good in themselves', but possible means to the realization of intrinsic goods.

Rationality is a property not just of ends but of means. How should individuals and governments conduct themselves so as to maximize the production of good states of mind? Keynes's most general answer is given by his theory of probability, the subject of his *Treatise on Probability*, written before World War I but published in 1921. The relationship of this theory to Keynes's concept of rational economic behaviour in the *General Theory*, as well as to the theory of rational expectations, has been expertly analysed by Dr Rod O'Donnell (1989). The problem with which Keynes started to grapple in 1904 is inherent in any consequentialist theory which takes seriously the problem of maximizing under uncertainty. How do we know what actions will best promote our purposes? Without an adequate basis for predicting the consequences of actions, utilitarian ethics is forced back to rule-consequentialism, the view that we should obey those rules which are generally followed or which would produce the best results if generally followed.

To avoid a conclusion which seemed to him to place an excessive premium on conventional behaviour, Keynes proposed probability as an intuited logical relationship between the factual premise and conclusion of an argument, warranting a degree of rational belief in the conclusion of interest. The field of rational action thus opened up beyond the availability of relative frequencies was, however, severely qualified by the principles of 'weight of argument' and 'moral risk'. By the first Keynes meant roughly the *amount* of evidence supporting a probability judgement. This does not alter the probability, but alters the amount of confidence it is rational to have in it. The principle of 'moral risk' suggests that it is more rational to aim for a smaller good which seems more probable of attainment than a larger good which seems less. Other things being equal, therefore, 'a high weight and the absence of risk increase *pro tanto* the desirability of the action to which they refer ...'.[17] The epistemological basis of Keynes's well-known bias towards short-termism and risk aversion was laid early in his life.

These principles are applicable to both private and public action, meaning by the latter the actions of public bodies. In general, Keynes accepted the Benthamite conclusion that egoism is superior to altruism as a maximizing principle.[18] This is because one has no direct knowledge of any state of mind but one's own. This is Keynes's main justification for organizing production on the basis of private property and the market system.

This pro-capitalist argument applies equally to the hedonistic and ideal versions of utilitarianism. However, there is a moral precriptivism in Moore lacking in Bentham, which arises from the central issue which Moore's ethics raises concerning the connection between goodness and wealth. The economist is not entitled to treat revealed private preferences as measures of goodness, because of such preferences one can still always ask: are they good? Nor can it be readily assumed that what is desired is ethically desirable. The view that people are ethically better off by being better off materially is self-evident only to a hedonist. Secondly, the focus on states of mind as a measure of goodness draws attention to the conflict between the states of mind required for economic gain, involving 'love of money' and economic calculation, and those required for the enjoyment of ethical goods. Most of Keynes's overt ethical reasoning in economics centres on these two questions.

The philosophical groundwork for his belief that the economist must interest himself in the composition of demand was laid as early as 1905 when he wrote that practical ethics should concern itself 'with the means of producing (a) good feelings, (b) fit objects ...'.[19]

Part of this programme, education for example, obviously falls outside economics. But economic action can create 'fit' objects for contemplation. Architecture was the main area to which Keynes looked to affect the composition of demand, both as a private individual (through building the Arts Theatre in Cambridge) and as the virtual creator and first Chairman of the Arts Council. Near the bottom of the Depression he said:

> ... Why not pull down the whole of South London from Westminster to Greenwich and make a good job of it – housing in that convenient area near to their work a much greater population than at present, in far better buildings with all the conveniences of modern life, yet at the same time providing hundreds of acres of squares and avenues, parks and public spaces, having, when it was finished, something magnificent to the eye, yet useful and convenient to human life, as a monument to our age.[20]

And in an article in *The Listener* of 4 April 1943 entitled 'How Much Does Finance Matter?' he wrote:

> I should like to see the war memorials of this tragic struggle take the shape of an enrichment of civic life of every great centre of population. Why should we not set aside, let us say, £50 millions a year for the next twenty years, to add in every substantial city of the realm the dignity of an ancient university or a European capital to our local schools and their surroundings, to our local government and its offices, and above all perhaps to provide a local civic centre of refreshment and entertainment with an ample theatre, a concert hall, a dance hall, a gallery, a British restaurant, canteens, cafes, and so forth.[21]

The ethical aim of these architectural projects was to increase the quantity of goodness, according to the principle of organic unity, by creating 'fit' objects for human use and contemplation. Creating, and sponsoring the creation of, beauty was the arena of action in which it was easiest for Keynes – and perhaps for any follower of Moore – to treat oneself as both end and means.

More interesting is Keynes's moral disquiet at the effect of *money-making* on character. This provokes his fiercest denunciations of capitalism – his depiction of the 'money-motive' as 'a somewhat disgusting morbidity, one of those semi-criminal, semi-pathological propensities which one hands over with a shudder to the specialists in mental disease';[22] his odd notion that the Jews had 'sublimated immortality into compound interest'[23] and his briefly held view that Soviet Russia was religious because it had made illegal the personal pursuit of profit.[24]

Keynes used three arguments in favour of economic progress as a means to goodness. First, an increase in material comfort is associated with an increase in 'fit' (that is, aesthetically and intellectually pleasing) objects, and thus conducive to good states of mind. Rich homes can afford beautiful pictures and furniture; rich states, beautiful theatres, universities, buildings. Secondly, an increase in material comfort is justifiable if it does not positively decrease ethical goodness, since a state of affairs in which people are good and happy may reasonably be judged better than one in which they are good and unhappy. In other words, the onus should be placed on opponents of material progress to show that it decreases the sum of ethical goodness.[25] Finally, Keynes argued, notably in his essay 'Economic Possibilities for our Grandchildren' (1930), that the freeing of mankind from pressing economic care would increase the *time* available for cultivating good states of mind (contemplation).

This is the nub. For Keynes, the positive ethical effect of material progress lay very largely in the increase in leisure which it made possible. There is no doubt that he wanted to get economic growth over with as quickly as possible, so that the 'money-motive', economic calculation, and with them economics which 'overvalues the economic criterion' for action, could disappear. Economics in its technical aspect was obliged to treat scarcity rather than fitness as the measure of wealth and welfare. Keynes found the calculating spirit equated by Robbins with economic rationality aesthetically and ethically distasteful: 'We destroy the beauty of the countryside because the unappropriated splendours of nature have no economic value. We are capable of shutting off the sun and the stars because they do not pay a dividend'.[26] The irony of the *General Theory* was that not only was calculation unethical, but it was more often than not irrational.

But there was no remedy for economizing until scarcity in relation to wants had been overcome. This could come about either by increasing the flow of income or by reorienting wants such that less income was required to satisfy them, or by a mixture of both.

Keynes's emphasis on maintaining a high level of investment thus serves an ethical as well as a technical purpose. Investment determines income, and therefore the standard of living, and through this has a major influence on the value of life, through its effect on the division of life between work and leisure. But the ethical inspiration of his economic theory comes out even more strikingly in a letter he wrote to T.S. Eliot in 1945:

> ... the full employment policy by means of investment is only one particular appli-
> cation of an intellectual theorem. You can produce the result just as well by consuming
> more or working less. Personally I regard the investment policy as first aid. In the
> US it almost certainly will not do the trick. Less work is the ultimate solution (a 35
> hour week in US would do the trick now). How you mix up the three ingredients of
> a cure is a matter of taste and experience, i.e. of morals and knowledge.[27]

The discussion so far has not explicitly considered Keynes's view of the role of the state in economic life. In his undergraduate essay on Burke, Keynes rejected any ethical or theocratic theory of the state. The proper aims of political action are the creation of what John Rawls later called 'primary goods' – those generally necessary for carrying out individual plans. Keynes comments approvingly on Burke's political theory:

> He did not much believe political ends good intrinsically ... The happiness of the people
> was his goal, and the science of government worthless except in so far as it guided

him to that end. Whatever the doctrines of utilitarianism may be worth abstractly ... they do not offer an unsatisfactory basis to a political theory. The tastes and emotions, good feeling and right judgment, these government cannot directly do much to foster and develop on any scheme or theory. Physical calm, material comfort, intellectual freedom are amongst the great and essential means to these good things; but they are the means to happiness also, and the government that sets the happiness of the governed before it will serve a good purpose, whatever the ethical theory from which it draws its inspiration.[28]

One finds little explicit discussion in Keynes about the economic duties of the state. He had no theory of public goods. His view of the boundary between private and public action was essentially pragmatic, varying with the requirements of contentment and equity in the given conditions. His best-known statement comes in his essay 'The End of Laissez-Faire'.

We cannot therefore settle on abstract grounds, but must handle on its merits in detail what Burke termed 'one of the finest problems in legislation', namely, to determine what the State ought to take upon itself to direct by the public wisdom, and what it ought to leave, with as little interference as possible, to individual exertion ... Perhaps the chief task to economists at this hour is to distinguish afresh the *Agenda* of government from the *Non-Agenda* ... The most important *Agenda* of the State relate not to those activities which private individuals are already fulfilling, but to those functions which fall outside the sphere of the individual, to those decisions which are made by *no one* if the State does not make them. The important thing for government is not do things which individuals are doing already, and to do them a little better or a little worse; but to do those things which at present are not done at all.[29]

This was written in 1926, but the same thought is contained in the *General Theory* when Keynes writes that his main purpose was to fill in the gaps in the 'Manchester system'. In the same passage he lauded, in almost Hayekian vein, individualistic capitalism as embodying 'the most secure and successful choices of former generations', and being 'the most powerful instrument to better the future'.[30]

In 'The End of Laissez-Faire' Keynes gives the state three economic duties: to control currency and credit, and collect and disseminate business facts; to balance saving and investment; and to control the size and quality of the population.[31] The first two lie at the heart of the Keynesian Revolution. They were designed to remedy the evils arising from 'risk, ignorance, and uncertainty' and to stabilize the level of employment. Keynes never really explained why the 'reasonably satisfactory average level' of employment attained under *laissez-faire* in the 19th century[32] was not reproduced between the two World Wars. The neo-Malthusian reference to population policy reflects Keynes's lifelong concern that technical progress should be used to increase leisure, not to support increased numbers.

Justice

Keynes regarded justice in distribution as making a necessary contribution to good states of mind, and looked to the state to secure it. But it is important to recognize that he rarely used the term in its familiar modern sense of social justice, that is, equality. His preferred term was 'equity'. Thus in the last chapter of the *General Theory* he referred to the 'arbitrary and inequitable distribution of wealth and incomes' in modern society. The equalitarian emphasis he gave to the concept of equity in this chapter reflects his new theoretical insight that growth is caused by investment not saving, and that 'thriftiness' retards the growth of wealth in any situation short of full employment. This justifies shrinking the share of income going to the *rentier*, or saving class, by redistributive taxation and by fixing a permanently low rate of interest.

His economic motive for advocating the 'euthanasia of the *rentier*' was to remove the power of the saver to exploit the scarcity value of capital. The possibility of his doing so was opened up by Keynes's liquidity preference theory of the rate of interest. The premium commanded by liquidity allows the *rentier* a reward for parting with money greater than his contribution to production. The liquidity preference theory has its roots in that half-submerged strand in Keynes's economics which relates economic malfunction to disturbance in just proportion. In correspondence, Keynes emphasized the equivalence of his theory with the medieval doctrine of usury, regretting that a work on the subject by a Jesuit, Father Watt, had not 'kept to the scholastic lingo, as phrases like *lucrum cessans* and *damnum emergens* ... [bring out] the main point ... viz., that ... it is usury to extract from the borrower some amount additional to the true sacrifice of the lender ...'.[33]

The foregoing discussion brings out the conventional inspiration of Keynes's concept of equity. A just distribution of income was one proportioned to economic contribution rather than to need. Keynes took the standard liberal view that the main distortion of long-run equity in distribution was the inheritance of wealth. So he favoured inheritance taxes. But he also used the word in a conservative sense as the absence of arbitrary interference with settled norms and expectations. By 'arbitrary' interferences he chiefly meant the windfall gains and losses associated with the business cycle or produced by government policies of inflation or deflation. This was very much the Burkean concept of equity – one related to what is considered 'fair' at any time, rather than to the abstract idea of justice. Keynes's consistent advocacy of price stability was heavily influenced by considerations of this kind. Guaranteeing equity in distribution in this sense is one of the explicit goals of macroeconomic stabilization.

Even more tellingly, Keynes rejected the scientific pretensions of welfare economics. Keynes's hostility to the welfare economics of his day has much to do with its dependence on hedonism and on the 'Benthamite arithmetic' which he regarded as hocus-pocus. This comes out in a letter he wrote to Abba Lerner in 1944, after he had read the latter's *Economics of Control*. Lerner had advanced the standard argument for income equality based on the application of the law of diminishing marginal utility to comparable quantities of satisfaction:

> There is only one chapter, chapter 3, where you fall flat-footed to the level of the vulgar. The whole complication and fascination (and truth) of the ethical doctrine of organic unity passes you by, and you accept uncritically the Benthamite arithmetic which I thought had been riddled to death forty years ago. It is one more proof of a grievous deficiency in the Cambridge curriculum as it was in your days with us ... For, I, two generations before, had been properly brought up and had spent endless hours on all this.[34]

Conclusion

I have tried to show that the principles of rational economic behaviour in Keynes all have reference to both theoretical and practical ethics. That's why it is justifiable to speak of his economics as applied ethics.

The Marshallian attempt to moralize Ricardian political economy has some parallel with efforts today to 'moralize' the political economy of Ronald Reagan and Margaret Thatcher. What has been lost is the sense that economists should or can be at the centre of such efforts, since ethics – except perhaps at Oxford – has no point of entry into the training of the modern economist.

J.N. Keynes, Maynard Keynes and, more doubtfully, Lionel Robbins, agreed that the economist should be trained in a moral science framework – that is, that a large part of his education should be additional to the specialized logical technique distinctive to economics. The father's view of the economist as a many-sided practitioner is echoed in the son's famous description of the 'master economist' as one who must 'possess a rare *combination* of gifts. He must ... be mathematician, historian, statesman, philosopher – in some degree ... No part of man's nature or his institutions must lie entirely outside his regard'.[35]

Since Keynes's day the weakness of ethics has given the social science disciplines their autonomy. This is associated with a collapse of confidence by the clerisy in its right to proclaim standards. For the clerisy of Keynes's day, wealth accumulation for its own sake was regarded as vulgar and silly. Perhaps the renewed intellectual vigour of ethics combined with growing environmental concerns will clothe the dry bones of formal economics with fresh human substance. At the very least the time may be ripe to consider anew the question of how economists should be trained to talk sensibly about the problems of our planet.

Notes

1. All references to Keynes's published works are to the Royal Economic Society's edition of *The Collected Writings of John Maynard Keynes*, hereafter *CW*. Keynes's unpublished papers are held at King's College, Cambridge, hereafter KP.
2. John Maynard Keynes to W. Temple, 3 December 1943, KP: General Correspondence.
3. *My Early Beliefs*, 9 September 1938, *CW*, x, p. 446.

4. Schumpeter (1952) p. 52.
5. Ibid., p. 60.
6. John Maynard Keynes to R.F. Harrod, 16 July 1938, *CW*, xiv, p. 300.
7. J.N. Keynes, op. cit., p. 2.
8. Robbins (1935) 2nd edition, p. 16.
9. Ibid., p. 24.
10. Ibid., p. 30.
11. Ibid., p. 91.
12. Ibid., p. 145.
13. Ibid., p. 148.
14. Towards the end of his life, Robbins retreated from the position of his essay, at least seman-tically. He proposed to revive the term 'political economy' to cover that part of 'our sphere of interest which essentially involves judgments of value'. (T. Ely Lecture, 1981; reprinted in the 3rd edition of *Nature and Significance*, 1984, p. xxvii). His 'political economy' is thus the same as J.N. Keynes's 'applied economics', in which economic science furnishes only one of the criteria for economic policy. But because his definition of the subject matter remains quite different from J.N. Keynes's, economics and political economy remain, for Robbins, in juxtaposition rather than being linked. This is made clear when Robbins proposes that instruction in economics 'will be more fruitful if, side by side, they [*sic*.] run parallel with suitable courses in Politics and History ...' (p. xxxi).
15. John Maynard Keynes to R.F. Harrod, 4 July 1938, *CW*, xiv, p. 297.
16. Moore (1959) pp. 188–9.
17. J.M. Keynes, *A Treatise on Probability*, 1921, *CW*, viii, p. 348.
18. 'Egoism', a paper read to the Apostles on 26 February 1906, KP: UA/26.
19. 'Miscellaneous Ethica', July–September 1905, KP: UA/21.
20. 'Saving and Spending', 14 January 1931, *CW*, ix, p. 139.
21. KP: A/42.
22. 'Economic Possibilities for our Grandchildren', October 1930, *CW*, ix, p. 329.
23. 'Einstein', 22 June 1926, *CW*, x, p. 383.
24. 'A Short View of Soviet Russia', *CW*, ix, pp. 259–61.
25. See Skidelsky (1992) pp. 65–6.
26. 'National Self-Sufficiency', July 1933, *CW*, xxi, pp. 65–6.
27. John Maynard Keynes to T.S. Eliot, 5 April 1945, *CW*, xxvii, p. 384.
28. 'The Political Doctrines of Edmund Burke', November 1904, pp. 16–17, 95. KP: UA/20.
29. 'The End of Laissez-Faire', July 1926, *CW*, ix, pp. 289–91.
30. *The General Theory of Employment, Interest and Money*, 1936, *CW*, vii, pp. 370–71.
31. *CW*, ix, p. 289.
32. *CW*, vii, p. 307.
33. John Maynard Keynes to Cornelius Gregg, 9 April 1946. KP: General Correspondence.
34. John Maynard Keynes to Abba Lerner, 27 September 1944, KP: L/44.
35. 'Alfred Marshall', 1924, *CW*, x, pp. 173–4.

References

Keynes, J.N. (1891), *The Scope and Method of Political Economy*, London: Macmillan.
Moore, G.E. (1959), *Principia Ethica*, Cambridge: Cambridge University Press.
O'Donnell, R.M. (1989), *Keynes: Philosophy Ethics and Politics*, London: Macmillan.
Rees-Mogg, W. (1983), 'Confessions of a Justified Monetarist', in *The Times*, 10 November.
Robbins, L. (1935), *An Essay on the Nature and Significance of Economic Science* (2nd edition), London: Macmillan.
Schumpeter, J.A. (1952), 'John Maynard Keynes', in *Ten Great Economists*, London: Allen & Unwin.
Skidelsky, R. (1992), *John Maynard Keynes* (vol. 2), London: Macmillan.

8 Ethical constraints on price flexibility
Massimo M. Beber and Lorenzo Ornaghi[1]

Introduction

A not altogether parodistic characterization of the orthodox relationship between the price system and ethics sees the former as pure means – a mechanism for co-ordinating the actions of individual economic agents – while the latter intervenes to doctor market results in the interests of justice and fairness. This cosy division of labour between economists exploring the 'efficiency' of decentralized exchange within a full set of competitive markets, and policy-makers expressing a society's 'moral values' (motivations other than self-seeking) is becoming increasingly untenable. It was only feasible while the area of economic activity largely overlapped that of political jurisdictions. Ethics could then be superimposed upon market exchange as a limit: typically, the state would fine-tune the distribution of rewards produced by the market (a distribution which reflected the optimal use of all available resources) by taxing some incomes and adding to others (redistribution), by providing some goods and services at administered prices, some of which may be zero (public provision), and finally by limiting trading possibilities, for example in heroin (prohibition is equivalent to a price administratively set at infinity).

It is the coincidence between the domain of price-regulated relationships and common citizenship which is coming to a close, due to the phenomenon of international economic integration: indeed, the currently much-debated crisis of the state finds its deeper roots in this 'denationalization' of the economy. Economic integration is fast spinning a web connecting people once distant through price-defined relationships involving goods and services once technically unthinkable. Seen in this light, the neo-liberal agenda of the 1980s has been more a matter of letting the frontiers of the state be pushed back by the process of integration, rather than actively pushing them back.

What are the implications of these structural changes for the technocratic vision of flexible prices as a value-free mechanism for efficient allocation? As more and more economic relationships span national borders, it becomes progressively less feasible to legitimize the operation of the price mechanism from outside economics by means of a morality embodied in the state (whether as great administrator or supplier): the authority of one state no longer covers all the parties to the price-defined contract. Unable to shift responsibility for its ethical implications onto supranational political processes, the price system, in order to

101

co-ordinate the increasingly global network of production and exchange activities, needs to be seen as ultimately ethical in its operation.

The legitimacy of the market would unavoidably be challenged if it were perceived as conflicting with ethical values, or even just as alienated from them. Regarded as the consequences of predetermined inequalities in economic power, rather than as the preconditions for co-ordinating productive activity to the common advantage of all members of society, the price signals given by the market would be resisted. This implies an attack on the legal framework of property rights and rules of contract; either by individuals, in the form of law-breaking, or by the political process, in the form of anti-market law-making. The current advance of the market experienced across so many political systems would then be merely a Pyrrhic victory. Enormous opportunities for improved welfare through enlightened use of the market mechanism have only recently arisen in the former socialist block; the consequences of such a reversal are daunting to contemplate, and should give us the confidence of desperate necessity in our current 'essays in trespassing' on the disputed borderlands between ethics and economics.

Could the subcontracting of ethics to 'legitimate governments', which has characterized 20th century mixed economies, be replicated at the global level? That no supernational political structures exist, capable at least of sharing the ethical role historically performed by nation states, is painfully clear; not just in Bosnia or Somalia, but in the very serious problems which have beset what has been called the 'national management of the international economy'.[2]

Yet while advances in science as a technique of intervention steadily reduce the areas in which we can expect the consequences of our actions to boomerang on us, progress in our analytical knowledge of economic and social relationships makes us increasingly more aware of the ultimate interdependence of things. This actually reduces the need for 'hard-core altruism': to the extent that enlightened self-interest allows us to promote an international moral solidarity superseding economic nationalism, we shall be able to allow price flexibility its full informational role.

This chapter begins by examining the importance of the price mechanism in the analysis of market economies: different 'images' of price flexibility are extracted from the works of economists, with no pretence to exhaustiveness, but in an attempt to capture the essence of different visions of the market mechanism and of its relationship to ethics. The long process of autonomization of economics from ethics reached completion in the 'new classical' versions of general competitive equilibrium, which assumed away-market failure, just at the time when the credibility of the nation state as an expression of society's ethical values was being challenged vigorously, particularly from the theorists of public choice. As a result, the 1980s were characterized by a much stronger confidence in the market mechanism, seen both as intrinsically efficient and not passible of ethical improvement by means of a chimerical political morality. The pendulum, however, seems to be swinging back, as markets without ethics appear to impose painful and ultimately unsustainable strains on the social fabric of nation states and indeed on the network of relationships between them. It is unlikely that a new equilibrium between efficiency and ethics will be reached, however, if our institutional outlook is blinkered to the dichotomy between '(competitive) market' and 'nation state'; both of these concepts, in fact, are of diminishing relevance for an understanding of contemporary economic relationships, due to the combined effects of transformation in industrial structures and international economic integration. It is argued that the above dichotomy constitutes an oversimplification which must not be allowed to stifle the search for a new institutional framework of co-operation, just as in reality the nation state never held a monopoly as the institutional framework of the market system, being just one of many co-operative arrangements, and increasingly not even the dominant one. The proper role for social scientists starts therefore with pointing out how much of ethics can really be shown to represent no more than a fairness prerequisite to the shared exploitation of gains from co-operation which the price system fails to capture and to apportion fully. The ultimate analytical objective must be to devise models of international economic integration which make ethical behaviour attractive, by demonstrating the gains from co-operation; while at the applied level, the challenge is to explore possible modifications of existing institutions, or indeed the design of new ones, enabling such gains to be reaped.

Market mechanism ethics and the state

The first thing to realize is that the orthodox contemporary economist finds it rather difficult to identify an ethical dimension in the flexibility of prices.[3]

Over the last 20 years, the dominant explanation of how decentralized economies work has been based squarely on the tireless work performed by prices as 'indices of scarcity'. It is by telling the entrepreneur where to deploy both talent and resources, by telling the worker into which skills to retrain, by telling sixth-formers whether to choose arts or sciences, that the price system performs its priceless task; and it is only if all prices are free to move to reflect changes in supply and demand (that is, in effect, in the underlying 'deep parameters' of endowments and tastes) that the task can be performed over time.

In this perspective, a society's economic problem reduces to a system of simultaneous equations in which resources are matched not to needs (which are assumed to be infinite) but rather to effectual demands, that is, needs backed by purchasing power: the solution consists in a vector of prices that brings the supply and demand for each good and service into equilibrium, thus 'informing' the mutually consistent choices of all the agents in the economy.

The price mechanism as a benevolent 'invisible hand'
The intellectual paternity of this concept is usually attributed to Adam Smith's 'invisible hand'. Having pointed out that a merchant will prefer to employ his capital 'as near home as he can' (because of the better knowledge of people and of the legal system), and that 'it is only for the sake of profit that any man employs a capital', Smith concluded thus:

> ... every individual necessarily labours to render the annual revenue of the society as great as he can. He generally, indeed, neither intends to promote the publick interest, nor knows how much he is promoting it. By preferring the support of domestick to that of foreign industry, he intends only his own security; and by directing that industry in such a manner as its produce may be of the greatest value, he intends only his own gain, and he is in this, as in many other cases, led by an invisible hand to promote an end which was no part of his intention (Smith, 1976, p. 456).

In Smith, the 'ordinary or average rates' of wage, profit and rent make up 'what may be called its natural price':

> The natural price, therefore, is as it were, the central price, to which the prices of all commodities are continually gravitating. Different accidents may sometimes keep them suspended a good deal above it, and sometimes force them down even somewhat below it. But whatever may be the obstacles which hinder them from settling in this centre of repose and continuance, they are constantly tending towards it (Smith, 1976, p. 75).

Market prices need to fluctuate freely, so that the profit rates for different activities may signal over- or underemployment of stock in the particular trade: they provide the information actuating the force of competition, which will divert capital from (and thus reduce supply in) the overstocked markets:
The market price of any particular commodity:

> ... can seldom continue long below its natural price. Whatever part of it was paid below the natural rate, the persons whose interest it affected would immediately feel the loss, and would immediately withdraw either so much land, or so much labour, or so much stock, from being employed about it, that the quantity brought to market would soon be no more than sufficient to supply the effectual demand. Its market price, therefore, would soon rise to the natural price. This at least would be the case where there was perfect liberty (Smith, 1976, p. 79).

As capital provides the wage fund (that is, the effectual demand) for labour, the same mechanism of competition would repeat itself in the labour market, with workers being led from one industry to another by changes in the wage. Therefore in all markets, when the demand for a good exceeds the supply of it, a rise in the price of that good relative to its initial value will on the one hand stimulate supply, and on the other ration demand, with the process continuing until equilibrium between the two sides of the market is re-established: the convergent movements of quantities demanded and supplied along both blades of a Marshallian pair of scissors make up an image only marginally less well known than that of the invisible hand, and more appropriate to our specific theme. If this did not happen, it was due to the statutes of apprenticeship and other corporation laws, which led workers in declining trades to 'chuse to come upon the parish'; on the whole, Smith believed that labour as well as capital would respond to price signals, and his judgement of guilds and other 'restrictive practices' was correspondingly negative.

Not only was Smith aware that market prices could be quite some way away from their natural value; he also recognized that the process of gravitation would deliver only an approximation. There is a degree of indeterminacy in the process whereby each price:

> ... is adjusted, however, not by any accurate measure, but by the higgling and bargaining of the market, according to that sort of rough equality which, though not exact, is sufficient for carrying on the business of common life (Smith, 1976, p. 49).

The imprecision of such 'rough equality', however, would not have worried Smith unduly: in *The Wealth of Nations*, the analysis of the operation of the price mechanism constituted a crucial element for the interpretation of the historical dynamics of post-feudal economies, and the emphasis was on prices as incentives to change, rather than as determinants of a perfectly determined but static equilibrium.

This strong link between Smith's theory of the price mechanism and his teleological view of history implied that, for the Scottish economist and philosopher, ethics were not outside the market: even more dangerously for the contemporary economist, they were for him (as for Newton) religious ethics: the invisible hand which led the baker and the butcher really ultimately belonged to God.

In addition, Smith had already anticipated a theme – that of the deep connection between market and political freedom as a separate justification of the former's ethical value – which has been very often articulated since:

> The statesman, who should attempt to direct private people in what manner they ought to employ their capitals, would not only load himself with a most unnecessary attention, but assume an authority which could safely be trusted, not only to no single person, but to no council or senate whatever, and which would nowhere be so dangerous as in the hands of a man who had folly and presumption enough to fancy himself fit to exercise it (Smith, 1976, p. 456).

In this, Smith did not differ from a number of contributions to the theory of prices from the prehistory of economics. Ethics were glaringly obvious in many philosophers' reflections on the price system prior to the beginnings of classical political economy. Moral concerns prompted Aristotle's analysis of market exchange and of money in determining prices; and in the 13th century, Thomas Aquinas was led to the concept of 'just price' and to the condemnation of usury, by his intellectual quest for the ethics of the market-place.

Yet, as long as the 'market economy' only constituted a limited part of the social interactions within an agrarian, largely subsistence economy, profit-seeking in a context of negligible growth often appeared to produce one or many losers for every winner: it was then natural to see the role of prices in terms of the implied network of interpersonal relationships – with the obvious implication that the stability of such just prices was a desirable property. As to the determination of just prices:

> The best and safest way would be for the temporal authorities to appoint over this matter wise and honest men who would appraise the cost of all sorts of wares and fix accordingly the outside price at which the merchant would get his due and have an honest living.[4]

Custom would provide an alternative in the absence of such regulation, and the concept of 'honest living' provided a long stop when not even custom was at hand: for the founder of Reformation, profit-maximization was indeed sinful.

While the era of commercial capitalism, which prompted Smith's economic thinking, was characterized by efficient exchange and relatively slow accumulation, with the Industrial Revolution production took centre stage. What Smith had foreseen, Ricardo, Malthus, Marx and John Stuart Mill analysed in depth: this was the 'surplus approach' to economic activity, focused on the production of commodities by means of commodities and by the generation of an annual surplus available for accumulation and hence for the growth of the system.

When the Italian economist Piero Sraffa gave a formally precise representation of such a system, this consisted – with a superficial similarity to the general equilibrium approaches – of a system of simultaneous equations to be solved in prices. In Sraffa, however, the parameters of the system were not given endowments and individual tastes, but rather the characteristics of the technology of production (represented by the matrix of production coefficients) and either the wage rate or the profit rate. The difference could not be greater: demand plays no role (at least in the determination of the prices of basic commodities) and either the price of labour or the price of capital must be given from the outside.

For the classical economists, fluctuations in market prices do perform a useful function precisely because their ultimate resting point (the 'natural price', resulting from a convergent 'gravitation process') is not determined by supply and demand, but rather by value, a concept which Ricardo tried vainly to relate to the amount of labour which had gone into production.

Value-neutral market efficiency: a 'severed hand'?

It is really only much later, with the Marginalist Revolution of Jevons, Walras and Menger, that prices decisively shed their earlier ethical connotations.

Significantly, the new 'catallactics' (or economics of exchange) flourished, especially in countries (such as Britain) which were, in the last quarter of the 19th century, already experiencing an 'industrial climacteric' in which the rumbustious growth of earlier decades had settled into less rapid, but steadier, growth. Elsewhere, the attention of economists often concentrated on factors other than the functioning of the price system: in explaining its rapid industrialization, German economists for a considerable time eschewed price analysis in favour of descriptive and comparative studies of institutions: this was the historical School of Gustav Schmoller.

It was a rather forced interpretation of Adam Smith's thought – the price mechanism as a timeless co-ordination mechanism, rooted in formal modelling rather than history – which provided the pillarstone on which the grand edifice of economics as an autonomous discipline has been built. This process of theoretical development soon led to that definition of the discipline which we still absorb from the textbooks: economics as 'the science that studies the relationship between ends and means that have alternative uses' (Robbins, 1932, p. 27).

Eventually, this line of research gave us the theoretical achievement of a definitive statement of the theory of competitive markets; and to this day, modern general equilibrium theorists claim intellectual descent from Smith's analysis, as for example does Frank Hahn:

> There is by now a long and fairly imposing line of economists from Adam Smith to the present who have sought to show that a decentralized economy motivated by self-interest ... would be compatible with a coherent disposition of resources that could be regarded, in a well defined sense, as superior to a large class of possible alternative dispositions. ... It is important to understand how surprising this claim must be to anyone not exposed to this tradition. The immediate 'common sense' answer to the question, 'What will an economy motivated by individual greed and controlled by a very large number of different agents look like?' is probably: There will be chaos (Arrow and Hahn, 1971, pp. vi–vii).

Moreover, the order of the market suggested a separate role for ethics: general equilibrium theory having demonstrated the superiority of a decentralized economy in making the cake as large and thick as possible, its normative twin, welfare economics, studied the various ways to squabble about slices.

It is an oft-repeated but nevertheless important aspect of this process of gradual autonomization of economics from ethics, that it should have boosted the economic profession's self-esteem as a community of proper scientists. It is by no means accidental that this process should have coincided with the period of dominance of positivism as a methodological position.

Price flexibility was essential to the mathematical (hence presumably scientific) representation of the equilibrium states of the system. At the same time, the 'optimal' properties of the equilibria reached by the competitive system rendered ethical concerns about its operation apparently groundless: how could it possibly be wrong to make sure that the cake to be baked was as large as possible, at least as long as we could ensure that in the process nobody ended up with a smaller slice than before?

Of course, some 'special cases' did remain (public goods, merit goods and bads, monopolies), in which the results of an unhindered operation of the price mechanism were considered unethical; these 'market failures' were, however, widely accepted exceptions to the general rule of optimal allocation by price signalling, and they aroused relatively little controversy. The debate between the enthusiasts of public ownership of utilities and the advocates of privatization, for example, is a debate about means: both parties agree that the monopolistic price is unfair as well as inefficient and needs regulating to somewhere closer to its competitive value.

The view just presented implies a convenient linearity in the development of economic thought from the butcher and the baker to the terribly numerate auctioneer. Yet Sen has clearly shown how this is equivalent to attributing paternity to one severed limb, forgetting the ultimately religious justification of the coherence between self-love and general good.[5]

The welfare properties of competitive equilibrium
In the new vision, the essential function of prices (no longer 'values') is to provide a vector of 'indices of scarcity', which will guide individual choices in such a way as to make the best possible use of (by definition scarce) resources.

Economic agents – that is all of us in our capacity as producers and traders – are represented as 'coming to market' with our endowments, or bundle of goods and services with which we wish to trade. The applicable rates of exchange between any pair of such goods – their relative prices – are supposed to emerge somehow from a repeated process of trial and error, sometimes inelegantly called 'groping': one of the great architects of the general equilibrium approach, Leon Walras, idealized price formation in terms of an auctioneer announcing successive series of prices, adding up demands and supplies at those levels, then reducing the prices of those goods in excess supply and increasing those in excess demand, announcing the new prices, collecting the corresponding demands and supplies, and continuing the process until a set of prices is found for which all markets clear. For this process of tatonnement to succeed, it is necessary that the auctioneer be free to alter any price by any amount necessary to equate the demand and supply for that particular good. Note that the agents have no power to dictate prices, only to choose how much to trade at a given price; and that nobody is allowed to trade until the 'right' prices have been found and announced, and then only at those prices.

What can we say about the characteristics of the state thus arrived at? Welfare economists have proved two fundamental propositions: the first optimality theorem states that if a competitive equilibrium exists at all, and if all commodities relevant to costs or utilities are in fact priced in the market, then the equilibrium is necessarily optimal in the following precise sense (due to Vilfredo Pareto): there is no other allocation of resources to services which will make all participants in the market better off. The second optimality theorem says that if there are no increasing returns in production, and if certain other minor conditions are satisfied, then every optimal state is a competitive equilibrium corresponding to some initial distribution of purchasing power.[6]

This representation of the market process gives the price mechanism a most powerful role: it is indeed the supercomputer spewing out the right answers. The flexible prices of a competitive market system allow us, given our endowments of wealth and skills, to procure the 'best' consumption bundle available, in terms of our own tastes and those of our trading partners. 'Making the most of what we have got' hardly raises ethical issues: whatever our morals, we cannot object to optimal states in general. The market's role is both essential to the solution of the economic problem and fully free from any ethical considerations: this is the message of the first theorem. Incidentally, this decentralized co-ordination of the activities of large numbers of economic agents through the operation of the price system has often been extolled as an outcome that no purposeful, centralized system of planning could ever emulate. Yet progressively more precise statements of competitive general equilibrium have revealed how stringent the required assumptions really are; with the result that it is now considerably less obvious whether more assumptional heroism is required to postulate, for example, perfect knowledge, foresight and a full set of contingent future markets, than to swallow the concept of an omniscient and omnipotent planner.

Optimality ensures that no trading opportunities remain unexploited: but whoever comes to market empty-handed will go hungry. Thus any particular Pareto-optimal equilibrium may be unacceptable to us because it does indeed let some agents starve. Here, the second theorem reassures us that any optimal state (and we know we can only reasonably desire optimal ones) is a competitive equilibrium corresponding to some initial distribution of endowments: thus the way to feed the hungry is not by forcing other agents to pay more than they wish to for what they have to offer, but to increase what they have to offer before the auctioneer begins his job! To take but two implications of this vision, minimum wage legislation and fair rent laws should be superseded by some variant of 'negative income tax': asking individual employers or landlords to fund a society's moral values of a minimum acceptable standard of living, rather than spreading it universally through taxation, creates distortions without achieving its professed end.

There was a further strand in the ethical justification of price flexibility which the marginalist theories of competitive exchange were building. Darwin's theory of evolution (which had itself been inspired, according to its author, by a work of economics – Malthus's *Essay on the Principle of Population*) gave economists an impressive foundation for their ethical support of the invisible hand: the survival of the fittest in the natural world represented a constant improvement in living conditions, thus it was morally good. In Darwin's own words: '... as natural selection works only for the good of each being, all corporeal and mental endowments will tend to progress towards perfection' (Darwin, 1897, p. 47).

Overall, the result was a 'division of labour' between market and government, reflecting their belonging in the fields of 'resource optimization' and 'moral judgement', respectively.[7]

The ethics of inflation

Did the Keynesian Revolution upset the non-ethical vision of price flexibility introduced by marginalism perfected by Pareto and Walras? Keynes himself, as Gerald Shove's quip went, 'never took the twenty minutes necessary' to understand properly the theory of value.[8] His concern was with the relationship between the price level, the stock of money, what he insisted was 'the price of money' (the interest rate), and the real aggregates of output and employment. It was at this aggregate level of analysis that (not in Keynes himself, but rather in 'Keynesian Economics') there appeared for a time to emerge a different facet of the relationship between price flexibility and ethics. In the 1950s and 1960s, great store was put in the notion of a trade-off between the inflation rate and the level of unemployment. This relationship, known as the Phillips curve, was believed to allow the policy-maker a choice: as the shape of the curve tells us that it is possible to have full employment at some level of inflation, it must follow that inflation (unlimited upward flexibility of all prices) must be undesirable in its own right, and not as an obstacle to full employment of the resources of the economy. It might, of course, be argued that at a high inflation level 'noise' drowns out 'signal', with the resulting misallocation; but the relationship between aggregate inflation and relative price variability is a complex one, and does not lend itself to analysis within the Phillips curve framework. Thus it must be presumed that the undesirability of inflation was in the 'Robertson reason': the distortion of contracts entered into in the expectation of a stable price level.

There were in those years, particularly in the UK, various attempts at building a 'conflict theory of inflation', based upon a struggle between wage-bargainers and oligopolistic firms aiming to pass on increased labour costs; these could be construed as an attempt to recapture the ethical dimension of 'justice' (what capitalists and workers respectively perceive as 'belonging to them') in the explanation of price flexibility; significantly, most of the profession has since shied away from this direction of inquiry, ostensibly on the grounds that the measurement of conflict is too problematic.

At this junction I wish to mention a rather more subtle ethical implication of inflation, which was also studied by Dennis Robertson in the UK, and by a host of 'real trade-cycle theorists' on the Continent. On the assumption that workers' incomes are less flexible than profits, a rising price level will transfer resources to capitalists: these 'forced savings' may – through investment – allow the economy to grow faster than otherwise, while at the same time quite possibly reduce the standard of living – that is, of consumption – of the current generation in favour of future ones.

Yet Robertson himself foresaw that the potential for such 'well-meaning' redistributions to profit, of which Kaldor and other Keynesians were so fond in the early post-war years, would be eroded by offsetting behaviour on the part of those cheated by inflation. This was made clear by Robertson, with his unique blend of insight and humour:

> [inflation] is not as good fun as it used to be, for too many people have learnt to dodge its consequences. I am not sure that in Britain the day when the Church of England climbed onto the bandwagon by entering the market for ordinary shares will not be seen in retrospect to have signalized the end of 'a little inflation' as a respectable policy (Robertson, 1958, p. 13).

The point was, of course, that indexation mechanisms will gradually reduce inflationary redistribution.

Eventually, the whole notion of the trade-off was demolished in two successive assault waves. Milton Friedman showed how the trade-off could only persist while workers did not realize that inflation cut into their real wages; a decade later, Robert Lucas, having defined rationality as not being systematically fooled, having then assumed the world to be 'rational' in this sense, and furthermore that there exists a full set of competitive markets in which agents can operate, argued that the trade-off did not exist even in the short run. The 'ethics of inflation' were thus apparently laid to rest: inflation could not deliver the 'good' of more people in work, rather it would reduce our well-being somewhat.

The 1980s competitive experiment and the limits of the severed hand

This was the situation by the 1970s: but do we not have a paradox here? An interpretation of human economic activity giving pride of place to the impersonal, decentralized action of markets had come to dominate professional thinking at the end of a period of unprecedented growth, accompanied by unprecedented concentration in industry and intervention in the economy by governments.

It is necessary to distinguish two periods. In the 1950s and 1960s, pure theoreticians were relieved from the expectation that they should provide practical advice by the temporary domination of Keynesian policy-making: while the former analysed the dynamic and welfare properties of economies with perfectly flexible prices, the latter appeared prepared to consider the price level or its dynamics as a datum in the analysis. The completion of the research programme on full competitive equilibrium came at a time of crisis in the advice-giving branch of the profession: devoid of a simple answer to the breakdown of the Phillips curve, Keynesianism was replaced by the new classical macroeconomics which for the first time – even though their extreme confidence suggested otherwise – derived policy advice from the results of models in which all markets clear all the time.

Thus when market structures, both domestically and internationally, no longer bore much resemblance to the ideal type of perfect competition; and at a time when, following the first oil shock, the world economy entered a period of profound dislocation of its production structure, government advice was based, more explicitly than ever before, on models of pure exchange. The next decade – the 1980s – was indeed more a 'pure competitive' experiment than merely a monetarist one.

That the old equilibrium based upon an ever-increasing 'grants economy'[9] and the monetary validation of any wage and price dynamics had become untenable is undoubted. Have deregulation and liberalization been the answer?

The experience of the global economy since World War II has confirmed not only the enormous growth potential of increasingly integrated nation states, but also the possibility that – particularly in a period of relative stagnation, such as we have experienced since the early 1970s – global inequality may increase significantly. The OECD countries, with a fifth of world population, account for three-quarters of world output and four-fifths of world trade; both macroeconomic indicators[10] and other measures of standards of living (from malnutrition to infant mortality, and in some cases even life expectancy)[11] suggest that rather than 'trickling down', the top fifth's well-being is being accompanied by an erosion of living standards elsewhere. Moreover, this reverses the trend of the 1950s and 1960s.

Within the West, indifferent growth rates have been maintained in the presence of much larger unemployment and, by most measures, increased social conflict. As to the problems of market without a moral framework in the former East, abundant evidence – some of it presented elsewhere in this volume – is being accumulated in favour of the conclusion that it cannot possibly work.

Overall, the latest trend seems to be towards a rather more balanced assessment of the relationship between operation of the market mechanism, on the one hand,

and the purposeful pursuit of certain ethical requirements of social and political stability (both within countries and, crucially, in the relationships between them), on the other. Moreover, as existing supernational structures, from the United Nations to the European Union, strain under the weight of new responsibilities and appear to disappoint the high hopes placed in them, public opinion is increasingly tempted to turn to the 'traditional' outlets of ethical considerations, the nation states: yet are such intrinsically isolationist expectations realistic?

International economic integration and ethical 'openness'
National characteristics determine to a large extent the specific reaction of the 'body politic' to the malaise mentioned above. Underneath such diversity of forms, however, the state as ethical regulator of economic activity is seen everywhere as increasingly powerless. This suggests that it might be here – in the relationship between nation states and international market activity – that an explanation must be sought.

Since the end of World War II, national economies have become increasingly interdependent. A number of indicators (from the crudest one of trade openness, to the empirically problematic one of gross financial flows, to the correlation between domestic and foreign interest rates) show beyond doubt that more of our material well-being depends on economic transactions with foreigners than ever before, and even transactions with our fellow citizens are increasingly carried out at prices which reflect actions taken elsewhere: the price paid by British mortgage-holders (and not just while inside the ERM) is in some measure determined by decisions taken in Frankfurt, even if the funds lent are those deposited by fellow British citizens.

The end of national economic destinies
It befits the occasion for which this paper has been written – the Annual Meeting of the British Association for the Advancement of Science – that the theme to which we are led, in trying to analyse further the process of increasing interdependence, should be that of the accumulation of knowledge.

At the level of production, we notice that what is being traded is increasingly intellectual value-added, know-how: it is no longer physical goods, but rather embodied knowledge which drives the contemporary expansion of trade. Note, incidentally, that this 'de-materialization' of trade suggests that the current expansion is less likely to be reversed by a bottleneck in some crucial input: once the computer was invented, with its relatively trivial hardware requirements, trade in software expanded with no limit but the ingenuity of the programmers.

The 'knowledge professionals' belong to an emerging world social category characterized by an understanding, rooted in personal experience, of the interdependence of economic activities across border (for one thing, their skills are usually easily exportable), and conversely by a lack of commitment to their territorial community. For this category, estimated to account now for one in five of the US workforce, Robert Reich has recently coined the term of 'symbolic analyst':

> Symbolic analysts solve, identify, and broker problems by manipulating symbols. They simplify reality into abstract images that can be rearranged, juggled, experimented with, communicated to other specialists, and then, eventually, transformed back into reality. The manipulations are done with analytic tools, sharpened by experience. The tools may be mathematical algorithms, legal arguments, financial gimmicks, scientific principles, psychological insights about how to persuade or to amuse, systems of induction or deduction, or any other set of techniques for doing conceptual puzzles (Reich, 1991, p. 178).

At the level of information, the relevant increases in human knowledge have been those in mass communication. Loyalty to place, originally expressed by Adam Smith in his avowed indifference to an earthquake in China, and restated by Samuel Brittan in his model of 'successive circles of feelings of obligation',[12] cannot remain unaffected by the inescapable, if superficial, familiarity with the living conditions of far wider circles of humanity. Indeed, the relationship between geographical proximity (the defining dimension of the nation state) and altruistic feelings becomes a very loose one within the so-called 'global village': untelevised London street children may come second in our sympathy to little Irma at the mercy of the shells pounding Sarajevo.

Thus as the range and volume of market transactions between 'foreigners' increases, we are more aware than ever before of the consequences of our actions on our market counterparts or indeed on third parties, wherever they may be: to eat hamburgers without thinking of the rain forest, or to turn up the heating without picturing Norwegian forests decimated by acid rain, is becoming increasingly difficult.

The end of the auctioneer

A crucial characteristic of the increased interdependence between national economies is that it is led not by the anonymous actors of a set of competitive markets, but rather (with the only partial exception of trade in some staple commodities) by the very visible hand of multinational corporations. In some cases, exchanges between plants or subsidiaries of multinational enterprises now account for nearly one-half of international trade: these exchanges take place at administratively set 'transfer prices', whose determination represents a highly specialized managerial function.

Of course, within national economies, 'concentration of industry' goes back as far as the 'trustification' of heavy industries organized in the United States by Pierpont Morgan and the other great financiers of the end of the last century. Since then, prices have increasingly been made in the planning departments of large corporations, rather than being delivered by a fictional – and impartial – auctioneer.[13] In principle, this 'personification' of the auctioneer's price-making function in the relevant planning departments of a number of multinational corporations struck at the heart of a well-known defence of the market mechanism on moral grounds: its impersonality as a guarantee of fairness. In the general context of distribution, John Stuart Mill had observed:

> A fixed rule like that of equality, might be acquiesced in, and so might chance or an external necessity; but that a handful of human beings should weigh everybody in the balance, and give more to one and less to another at their sole pleasure and judgement, would not be borne unless from persons believed to be more than men and backed by supernatural principles (Mill, 1965, Book I, Ch. 2, Para. 4).

Later, Friedrich von Hayek spelt out the same concept with specific reference to the operation of the price mechanism:

> It is significant that one of the commonest objections to competition is that it is 'blind'. It is not irrelevant to recall that to the ancients blindness was an attribute of their deity of justice. Although competition and justice may have little else in common, it is as much a commendation of competition as of justice that it is no respecter of persons (Hayek, 1976, p. 76).

Under modern pricing conditions, however, the price-setters, no longer blind, need to be seen to be just. Yet while price-setting firms and price-taking consumers operated within one and the same country, this is precisely what a 'mixed economy' appeared to achieve: a combination of competition policy and fiscal redistribution seemed to provide a reasonable approximation to the competitive optimum, doctored where deemed necessary on grounds of fairness. This era was represented in the USA by Charles Erwin Wilson (GM Chairman and Secretary of Defense under Eisenhower) claiming that:

> I cannot conceive of one [conflict of interest] because for years I thought what was good for our country was good for General Motors, and vice versa. The difference did not exist. Our company is too big. It goes with the welfare of the country (quoted in Reich, 1991, p. 48).

The necessity and feasibility of institutional innovation

Nations, however, no longer 'rise and fall together', or more precisely with the fortunes of their large-scale industries; indeed, the globalization of production makes it harder to define which industries are in any sense 'theirs'.

Within each country, the labour force is breaking up into two segments: the unskilled and the cosmopolitan 'global symbolic analysts' who realize the self-defeating destiny of isolationist thinking – but precisely for this reason, no longer feel the same 'loyalty to place'. If indeed justice and fairness are only learnt by the sharing of a common history, culture and fate, then the gradual dilution of these bonds will render economic self-interest unbounded:

> ... while a cosmopolitan view provides a useful and appropriate perspective on many of the world's problems and avoids the pitfalls of zero-sum thinking, it may discourage the very steps necessary to remedy the problems it illuminates. It is not clear that mankind is significantly better off with an abundance of wise cosmopolitans feeling indifferent or ineffective in the face of the world's ills than it is with a bunch of foolish nationalists intent on making their particular society Number One (Reich, 1991, p. 311).

There is no market price for the development and market research that a Japanese car manufacturer performs in the USA; among other consequences, accepting the foreign owner's estimate of what such work is worth tends to result in rather less tax being paid in the USA than one might wish. Trust and co-operation are required if the economies of scale of mass production are to be exploited (internalized within a firm);[14] the transfer pricing problem is just one instance of the additional complications introduced in the distribution of the gains from co-operation when they must be shared across national borders.

This is particularly crucial in those economic relationships (between North and South, and between West and liberated East) characterized by large inequalities of economic power between the two groups interacting. The 'balance of terror' has been swept away, and the 'equilibrium of the market-place' is coming into its place: yet no such equilibrium, which is perceived as unjust, is feasible without coercion.

If we were to accept the view that 20th century capitalism could allow the price mechanism to work by delegating to the nation state the expression and implementation of each society's ethical concerns, then interdependence would necessarily be an unstable process and eventually reverse, in the absence of correspondingly wider regional and possibly world institutions, into an isolationist spiral (the experience of the inter-war period is often quoted in this respect).

Yet political science has shown that the 'crisis of the state' is a process some fundamental traits of which have been apparent at least since the end of the last century. Far from being the result of a dichotomic division of labour between 'state' (the place of ethics) and 'market' (the place of efficiency), the success of decentralized economies has been underpinned by an increasingly complex network of institutions including not just unions and large firms, but interest groups with disparate common denominators (including semi-legal or even criminal ones). Alfred Marshall caught this transformation with clarity even as it was just beginning:

The nation used to be called the 'Body Politic'. So long as this phrase was in common use, men thought of the interests of the whole nation when they used the word 'Political' and then 'Political Economy' served well enough as a name for the science. But now 'political interests' generally mean the interests of only some part or parts of the nation; so that it seems best to drop the name 'Political Economy' and speak simply of Economic Science, or more shortly Economics (quoted in Deane, 1989, p. 119).

In other words, market societies have long used their freedom to experiment with new forms of co-operative behaviour. Some were more effective than others: the corporatist experiment of the 1950s and 1960s did not achieve a permanent transformation in the confrontational approach in British industrial relations; on the other hand the science park movement, pioneered at Cambridge, has been a success based on 'enlightened self-interest'.

Conclusions

Can we as social scientists facilitate solutions based on altruism of the 'hard-core' variety? We strongly doubt it. Our challenge, it seems to us, is that of improving our analysis of integration (the theoretical dimension of knowledge) so as to reflect the expansion in human technical knowledge which constantly increases interdependence (by opening up new profitable opportunities for international relationships): this will mimimize the need for 'hard-core altruism' in making such interdependence sustainable.

The technology of production and exchange allows us to modify our own material environment more significantly than ever before, and for a larger proportion of humankind than ever before. It is essential that our models of economic behaviour should reflect this: tipping a restaurant waiter in Stoke-on-Trent would indeed have been ultimately altruistic when the trip from Cambridge took days; it may, however, be no more than far sighted self-interest under modern transport conditions, which make it all in all considerably less unlikely that we might be back.

At a rather more significant level of interdependence, to anchor the flexibility of exchange rates so as to avoid major dislocations in the traded sector of our own and our partners' economies represents a reasonable area for co-operative behaviour; but to have central bankers alone co-operate, while the fiscal arm of government follows purely domestic priorities, constitutes the wrong strategy.

Similarly, in the field of North–South and West–East relationships, to ensure that the prices of both goods and of capital do not trigger adjustment by massive migration is equally sensible; in this case, however, the answer may require co-operative behaviour not just or even mainly on the part of governments, but rather of the multinationals whose production and investment choices play such a crucial role in the developing country's long-term ability to pay its own way.

By achieving a better understanding of interdependence (and thus of the long-run consequences of our actions on ourselves through their effect on others) in these as in other areas, we can show the necessity of a co-operative framework for global market activity. The more successful we are in fostering such self-interest correctly understood, the less black all of our skies will be with chickens coming home to roost.

Notes
1. We thank Geoff Harcourt and Micá Panić for suggesting a number of improvements to an earlier version of this chapter.
2. See Panić (1988).
3. On the ethical dimension of economic behaviour, and on the purposeful distancing of economics from ethics, see Sen (1987).
4. Martin Luther, quoted in Deane (1989) p. 2.
5. See Sen's contribution to the present volume.
6. See Arrow (1963) pp. 942–3.
7. In such a world '... a most preferred social state can be achieved, with resource allocation being handled by the market and public policy confined to the redistribution of money income' (Arrow, 1963, p. 943).
8. The quip is alive and well in Cambridge oral folklore, although I have not been able to ascertain whether Shove wrote it or merely said it. On Keynes's lack of interest in the theory of value see also Kaldor (1980) p. 227.
9. On the concept of the 'grants economy' see Matthews and Stafford (eds) (1982). As the editors point out in their introduction, the fiscal difficulties of the time often slanted the analysis: 'Preoccupation with control of expenditure, however necessary, tended to produce a one-sided bias, such as might be produced if one thought of the price mechanism merely as a device to keep *down* consumption' (p. xv).
10. These are, in many ways, the least satisfactory measures of standard of living differentials because, for a variety of reasons, they systematically overestimate the gap between the rich and poor countries. See International Monetary Fund (1993), in which the use of more appropriate weightings increases the developing countries' share in world output from 17.71 per cent to 34.38 per cent (p. 117). This bias does not affect our observation, which is based upon trends rather than absolute levels.
11. United Nations (1990) pp. 202–21, 285–97.
12. See Smith (1976) p. 136 and Brittan (1971) p. 340.
13. On these developments, and on the parallel trend away from the competitive ideal type in labour markets, see Sylos-Labini (1993) pp. 313–19.
14. See Sen's contribution to the present volume.

References
Arrow, K.J. (1963), 'Uncertainty and the Welfare Economics of Medical Care', *American Economic Review*, **53**, 941–73
Arrow, K.J. and Hahn, F.H. (1971), *General Competitive Analysis*, Edinburgh: Oliver and Boyd.
Brittan, S. (1971), 'Morality and Foreign Policy in Capitalism and the Permissive Society' in *Capitalism and the Permissive Society*, Basingstoke: Macmillan.
Darwin, C. (1897), *The Origin of Species by Means of Natural Selection, or The Preservation of Favoured Races in the Struggle for Life*, (6th edition), London: J. Murray.
Deane, P. (1989), *The State and the Economic System. An Introduction to the History of Political Economy*, Oxford: Oxford University Press.
Hayek, F.A. von (1976), *The Road to Serfdom*, London: Routledge and Kegan Paul.
International Monetary Fund (1993), 'Revised Weights for the World Economic Outlook', *World Economic Outlook*, May.

Kaldor, N. (1980), *Essays on Value and Distribution*, London: Duckworth.

Matthews, R.C.O. and Stafford, G.B. (eds) (1982), *The Grants Economy and Collective Consumption*, Basingstoke: Macmillan.

Mill, J.S. (1965), *Principles of Political Economy with Some of Their Applications to Social Philosophy*, (Collected Works of J.S. Mill edited by J.M. Robson, Vol. 2), Toronto: University of Toronto Press.

Panic, M. (1988), *National Management of the International Economy*, Basingstoke: Macmillan.

Reich, R.B. (1991), *The Work of Nations. Preparing Ourselves for 21st Century Capitalism*, New York: Simon and Schuster.

Robbins, L.C. (1932), *An Essay on the Nature and Significance of Economic Science*, London: Macmillan.

Robertson, D.H. (1958), 'Stability and Progress: the Richer Countries' Problem', in *Stability and Progress in the World Economy, The First Congress of the International Economic Association*, Basingstoke: Macmillan.

Sen, A.K. (1987), *On Ethics and Economics*, Oxford: Basil Blackwell.

Smith, A. (1976), *An Inquiry into the Nature and Causes of the Wealth of Nations*, Oxford: Clarendon Press (the Glasgow edition of the Works and Correspondence of Adam Smith).

Sylos-Labini, P. (1993), 'Long-Run Changes in the Wage and Price Mechanism and the Process of Growth', in Baranzini Mauro and G.C. Harcourt (eds), *The Dynamics of the Wealth of Nations. Growth, Distribution and Structural Change*, Basingstoke: Macmillan.

United Nations (1990), *Global Outlook 2000*, New York: United Nations.

9 Altruism, ethics and economics: the significance of non-egoistic preferences for economics
John Fender[1]

Introduction

The aim of this chapter is to examine some ways in which the existence of altruism is relevant for economics and the design of economic institutions. However, first of all, it considers the preliminary questions of how altruism should be defined and whether it exists.

It is commonplace in economics to assume that agents are selfish, so we are considering the relaxation of a very standard assumption, and this would seem to require some justification. We argue in the next section of this chapter that some behaviour might be regarded as genuinely altruistic. The remainder of the chapter is concerned with the implications of the existence of altruism. We shall be concerned with both positive and normative questions. The question of how the existence of altruism affects the behaviour of the economy – the positive question – is, of course, of interest. But there is also the normative question of whether a little more altruism, at the margin, would be beneficial. It might seem that the answer to this question is obvious – that of course things would be better if people were more altruistic, and a number of ways in which this may occur will be discussed. However, we argue that things may not be that simple and that it is possible that greater altruism may sometimes make things worse. Kolm (1983) compares an altruistic with an egoistic economy, and argues that there are reasons for believing the altruistic economy will be more efficient. This may be the case, but this conclusion is not too relevant for policy purposes; we are not faced with a decision between an altruistic and an egoistic economy, the question is rather to what extent we should encourage a somewhat greater degree of altruism in the current economy.

One or two further issues are discussed in the final section. We would emphasize that we do not want to argue that greater altruism is not desirable; the main point is that the situation is often complex and paradoxical things may (but not necessarily will) occur.

Altruism: definition and existence

It is a common and standard (but by no means universal) assumption in economic theory that agents are both egoistic and rational. For example, a consumer may be assumed to obtain satisfaction from just his own consumption of a number of different goods; his preferences are represented by a utility function and he seeks to maximize the value of this, that is, to make himself as well off as possible, subject to a budget constraint, which represents his consumption possibilities, as determined by his income and the prices of the goods in question. The rationality assumption implies that he succeeds in maximizing the utility function subject to the constraint; the appropriateness of this assumption, at least in certain circumstances, has often been questioned, but in this chapter we shall retain it. Our focus will instead be on the implications of relaxing the egoism assumption.[2]

An initial attempt at a definition of altruism might be that altruism occurs when an individual's utility depends positively on the well-being of some other agents in the economy. However, excluding perhaps a few saints, individuals are at least to some extent concerned with their own well-being as well. It is useful to have a term for the self-regarding component of an agent's preferences, and in this chapter we will use the term 'felicity' for such a purpose; so a felicity function might be postulated for an individual to represent the egoistic component of her preferences. For a complete egoist, felicity and utility will coincide (we take utility to be whatever the individual seeks to maximize). However, if an individual is not a complete egoist, other people's well-being will affect her utility at least to some extent. Following Sen (1990), we shall say that such an individual exhibits commitment if such an interdependence reflects ethical beliefs; the individual believes that she ought to value others' well-being to some extent. So we might say that an individual is altruistic if she exhibits commitment towards at least some other individuals in the economy.[3] Commitment is distinguished by Sen from sympathy, where concern for others directly affects one's welfare. So someone who gives money to charity because it makes her feel good is exhibiting sympathy (she would feel worse off were she not to give the money); if she gives the money because she considers it the right thing to do, it is a case of commitment.

A number of points might be made about the above formulation of altruism. Suppose the individuals towards whom altruism is shown are at least to some extent altruistic. Then the question arises as to whether we should model altruism as the entering of one individual's utility function as an argument into another's utility function, or whether it is the felicity function (as defined above) which enters, or whether it should be modelled in some other way (possibly by putting the other agent's consumption vector into the first agent's utility function). In the first case, the possibility of a 'hall of mirrors' effect emerges. Romeo and Juliet have (let us suppose) strongly interdependent utility functions. Juliet enjoys seeing a butterfly; Romeo's utility increases as a consequence, but this produces a further increase in Juliet's utility, and so on indefinitely. It is possible that utility could 'explode' to infinity. For this not to occur, it is necessary to place restrictions on an individual's utility functions (as in Bernheim and Stark, 1988, p. 1036). However, we can argue that modelling altruism in this way is less plausible if altruism reflects ethical considerations, so that altruism is modelled as other individuals' felicities entering one's utility function (this would rule out the 'hall of mirrors' effect). If Robin Hood gives money (stolen from the rich) to the poor because he believes it is right that he do so, it seems plausible to argue that it is their poverty which is the crucial motivating factor (and this would be most appropriately captured by their level of felicity). It may well be the case that the ethical beliefs of the recipients have no effect on his behaviour at all, and one would conjecture that this would also be so for many other cases of altruistic behaviour.

A related question arises with respect to policy-making; should the policy-maker seek to maximize the sum of utilities, or felicities, or what? One might concur with Hammond who argues (1987, p. 88) that putting utilities into the social welfare function would be inappropriate as it would involve double-counting; the poor would matter not just because of their own low level of consumption, but because of Robin Hood's concern for them as well. It is perhaps more plausible to contend that the policy-maker, if utilitarian, should be concerned with the sum of felicities.

It may be difficult to identify behaviour that is genuinely altruistic, once an intertemporal perspective is adopted. It is easy to think of examples of apparently altruistic behaviour; people give money to charities, do voluntary work, vote, rescue Jews from Nazis, man lifeboats, leave bequests to their children and so forth. But many examples of apparent altruism have egoistic explanations; giving to charity may be motivated by the esteem generated among one's peers or by the expectation of future benefits, and so forth. With sufficient ingenuity, almost any behaviour can be explained in egoistic terms (martyrs are maximizing their chances of bliss in the hereafter). But such an approach is not very fruitful and comes close to being tautological, explaining very little (can such theories explain when individuals will undergo martyrdom, how much they will give to charity, and so forth?).

I believe it plausible to contend that there is some human behaviour which may be described as genuinely altruistic. One compelling piece of evidence for this contention is to be found in the remarkable paper by Monroe *et al.* (1990), which is based on interviews with rescuers of Jews in Nazi-occupied Europe. A number of in-depth interviews were held; interviews were also held with what might be described as control groups. It seemed extremely difficult to explain the rescuers' behaviour in self-interested terms. Did they undergo the huge personal risks involved in rescuing the Jews because of expected rewards in the hereafter? Some of the rescuers had no religious beliefs. Was the motivation current pressure or future praise from family and friends? Some of the rescuers kept their activities secret from everyone whose knowledge was not essential for the success of the operation, and so on. The most reasonable explanation is that much of the rescue activity was motivated by genuinely altruistic concerns. It might be pointed out that such behaviour was (and is) fairly rare; however, it should be emphasized that the study considers behaviour that might be described as highly altruistic (often involving fairly immediate danger to life, and generating no conceivable personal benefits) and it is not surprising that this is exhibited only by a few. Many more people may be willing to incur smaller costs in order to help others (for example, being late for a date in order to save a life in the aftermath of a traffic accident), and most people are presumably altruistic towards at least some individuals (family members, friends, colleagues, clients, pupils, fellow citizens, and so on).

So, we take it that altruism exists when individuals exhibit commitment towards other individuals, and that some behaviour is indeed genuinely altruistic. Most of the remainder of this chapter is concerned with some of the implications of altruism; the next section considers some of the ways in which altruism might improve matters.

Why altruism might make things better
The prisoner's dilemma and altruism
A useful starting point for many discussions of societal arrangements is the well-known prisoner's dilemma; an example is given in Figure 9.1. There are two players, Row and Column, each of whom has a choice of two actions: R1 and R2 for Row, C1 and C2 for Column. The return each player receives depends on both players' actions, and this is illustrated in Figure 9.1; for example, if Row plays R2 and Column C1, Row receives 9 and Column 0, and so forth. The returns are measured in terms of whatever the agents are concerned about (money income, felicity?) and, in the basic form of the game, it is played just once, the players cannot communicate (so, *a fortiori*, they cannot enter into enforceable agreements specifying how each of them should play) and the players move simultaneously (so neither knows what the other has played when making his move).

		Column	
		C1	C2
Row	R1	5 , 5	0 , 9
	R2	9 , 0	1 , 1

Figure 9.1   The prisoner's dilemma

Suppose, initially, that the players are egoistic (that is, each cares solely about his own return). What happens? It seems that there is a well-defined solution. Row might reason as follows: 'if Column plays C1, then if I play R1, I get 5, whereas if I play R2, I get 9. However, if Column plays C2, then I only get 1 by playing R2 but this is better than the 0 I would get by playing R1; it follows that whatever my opponent plays, I'm better off playing R2'. Row therefore chooses R2. (If one player has a strategy which does better for him than any other strategy, regardless of what his opponent does, as is the case here, we describe it as his dominant strategy.) The game is symmetrical, so we would expect Column to choose C2 and the outcome of the game to be that given by the lower right box; this is a 'Nash equilibrium', where each player is doing as well as possible, given the choice of his opponent, and has no incentive to change his behaviour. However – and this is the crucial point – the outcome is worse for both of the players than if they had played R1, C1. In the latter equilibrium, both players receive 5, whereas in the Nash equilibrium each receives just 1.

There are many ways in which this basic game might be extended; we will mention two. One is to raise the number of players; this gives rise to what might be described as a many-person prisoner's dilemma and the same sort of Pareto inferior outcome (that is, one which is inferior for all players to another feasible outcome) emerges. Secondly, the basic game might be repeated a number of times (this gives rise to what is known as the temporally iterated prisoner's dilemma); there has been considerable discussion of the circumstances under which repetition is likely to lead to the attainment of the 'desirable' outcome, but this is not something we will pursue here.

Many societal problems have a structure similar to that of the many-person prisoner's dilemma; examples are congestion, financing public goods, voting and using more energy in a time of shortage. It might be thought that society can evolve mechanisms for resolving the problem, and, indeed, in many cases it has. We will discuss two possible solutions: taxing (or imposing penalties on) 'wrong behaviour' and altruism. Suppose the government imposes a tax of 5 units on both R2 and C2. Then we obtain the pay-off matrix given in Figure 9.2; it is easy to see that each agent's optimal strategy changes and the 'desirable

Column

		C1	C2
Row	R1	5 , 5	0 , 4
	R2	4 , 0	−4 , −4

Figure 9.2   Taxation and the prisoner's dilemma

outcome' (R1, C1) emerges. It seems then that the government may have a role in resolving prisoner's dilemmas and it is not too difficult to think of a number of examples (for example, guaranteeing property rights, imposing taxes to finance public goods, and so on).

However, whilst government intervention may be sufficient to resolve some prisoner's dilemma-type problems,[4] it may not be necessary. Altruism may do the job as well. Suppose that each agent is altruistic, and puts the same weight on the other person's felicity as on his own. Then, assuming that the entries in Figure 9.1 are the agents' felicities, altruism converts the matrix of returns specified in utilities (which is what agents seek to maximize) into that given in Figure 9.3. (So each agent is indifferent between his getting 9 units of felicity and the other person nothing and the reverse; this is obviously an extremely high degree of altruism.) It is apparent that the dilemma is resolved; the one Nash equilibrium is now the socially optimal outcome, that represented by the upper left-hand entry in the matrix.

Column

		C1	C2
	R1	5 , 5	4.5 , 4.5
Row			
	R2	4.5 , 4.5	1 , 1

Figure 9.3   Altruism and the prisoner's dilemma

Altruism with imperfect (asymmetric) information
Consider the following situation. Suppose a commodity is sold on a market; the quality of the commodity cannot be observed perfectly by buyers at the time of purchase; sellers do, however, know the quality of the product (or at least know more about it than buyers). Examples might be used cars ('lemons' as in Akerlof, 1970) or blood (as in Titmuss, 1970). Then, with egoistic behaviour, we might expect a 'market for lemons' to develop, with the goods sold being predominantly of inferior quality. Suppose now that instead of the commodity being provided on a market, it is donated by individuals who do not receive payment for it; one would assume that the reason it is donated is because of altruism; the donors care about the well-being of the purchasers. Blood is an obvious example. Someone who donates blood because he cares about the well-being of the recipient will obviously not do so if he knows his blood is contaminated; one would therefore expect that commodities which are provided by altruistic givers would not be subject to the lemons problem, whereby the

quality of the product transacted is lowered. Might there not be a case for arranging for commodities which are subject to a problem of this kind to be provided voluntarily by unpaid donors rather than via a standard market? This is less straightforward than might appear at first and I will confine myself to making just a few relevant points. First, the question of what society gives up when altruism is used for this purpose needs to be considered. Would those who give blood altruistically have done other altruistic deeds had the opportunity for blood donation not been available? (Someone who gives blood may feel that he has 'done my good deed for the day'; in the absence of such an opportunity, he may have done another good deed.) Secondly, what adjusts to ensure equilibrium when the commodity is allocated altruistically? In a conventional market, it is of course the price that adjusts; increased demand leads to a higher price, which tends to dampen demand and increase supply, and so forth. With an altruistic adjustment mechanism, it might be that increased 'need' for donations is communicated in some way to potential donors who decide to give more; but this is very vague and one would wish for a more precise analysis of the mechanism and a comparison of how effective this adjustment mechanism is compared with the price mechanism. However, there does not seem to be any analysis in the literature along these lines.

In fact there seem to be three independent contentions to be distinguished:

1. Providing a commodity through altruistic giving may eliminate a lemons problem that would exist were the commodity to be provided commercially.
2. If a commercial market exists alongside the voluntary donation of a commodity, this will devalue voluntary donation, so less will be given.
3. The more opportunities there are for altruistic giving, the more altruism will develop in a society.

I believe the first proposition to be true, but am uncertain about the other two.[5] It might be added that altruism is not the only reason for voluntary donation; peer pressure might be another. So it is not necessarily the case that relying on donations eliminates a lemons problem.

Lemons-type problems are quite common; imperfect information is the usual state of affairs and asymmetric information almost as common. In order for markets to work at all, a considerable amount of consideration for others, honesty, trust and goodwill are required. Legally enforceable contracts are presumably a crucial underpinning of economic life; however, for the law to function, it is presumably necessary that many involved in the legal system are honest (particularly judges). So it might be argued that it is wrong to suggest a dichotomy between egoistically based allocation mechanisms (markets) and altruistically based allocation mechanisms (for which there is not such a readily available term). Both types of mechanism require a considerable amount of altruism to function. Perhaps we should say that for conventional markets, self-interested behaviour is appropriate subject to certain constraints, whereas there are some markets (perhaps not many) where self-interested behaviour subject to the relevant constraints does not produce the desired outcome (in the sense that allocation by non-price means would be superior). It might be argued that the reason the British mechanism for blood collection and distribution is superior to the American system (if, indeed, it is superior) is precisely because certain members of society do not possess the appropriate norms (that is, not to sell blood when you have had certain diseases). If all members of society had acted according to such norms, then presumably the market for blood would work efficiently. So the need for altruism here arises only because certain members of society are not altruistic, at least in this particular respect. Moreover, for the altruistic mechanism to work, it is necessary only that a small (but not insignificant) fraction of the population be altruistic. This illustrates an important point, to which we will return; altruism can have significant effects even if only a small percentage of the population is altruistic.[6]

In concluding this section, we would emphasize the following point: altruism, or at least behaviour according to certain moral rules and norms, may be particularly relevant in situations of imperfect (or, to be more precise, asymmetric) information. Indeed, it is difficult to see any role at all for some virtues (for example, honesty) in a world of symmetric information (that is, a world in which everyone possesses the same information).

Why altruism might make things worse (or be irrelevant)

Although it might seem almost self-evident that more altruism would be better than less, this is not necessarily the case; it is possible to give examples in which altruism may make things worse (or at least not make things better), in a sense which can be made more precise. In this section we will present and discuss some examples of this.

The altruist's dilemma

It was argued above that altruism can resolve prisoner's dilemmas, but it is not hard to construct what might be described as the altruist's dilemma. Consider Figure 9.4, which is derived by switching the entries for the rewards of the two players in Figure 9.2. As it stands, there is no dilemma; each player plays his dominant strategy (R1 and C1) and the most desirable outcome is attained. Now, however, suppose both players become perfectly altruistic, in the sense that they are concerned solely with what the other player receives. Then the game matrix becomes equivalent to that given by Figure 9.1, and there is a prisoner's dilemma (or perhaps an altruist's dilemma). So, pure selfishness results in both players being better off (evaluated in terms of their felicity functions) than pure altruism (perhaps this means that pure altruism is 'self-defeating', as in Parfit

(1984)). The reader can easily convince himself, however, that this is not the case for moderate degrees of altruism (for example, where both players put equal weights on their own as on the other player's felicity, we get a game equivalent to that given by Figure 9.3). It is not clear, however, how important the altruist's dilemma is in practice; there do not seem to be any plausible examples of it in the literature, and it is difficult to think of any.[7]

		Column	
		C1	C2
Row	R1	5 , 5	9 , 0
	R2	0 , 9	1 , 1

Figure 9.4   The altruist's dilemma

The significance of the first theorem of welfare economics for altruism
The first theorem of welfare economics (see, for example, Kreps, 1990, p. 199) states that a Walrasian equilibrium is Pareto-efficient. A Walrasian equilibrium is attained when all consumers maximize utility subject to their budget constraints, perfectly competitive firms maximize profits and all markets clear (in the sense that supply equals demand for all commodities except for commodities with zero prices, when supply must not be less than demand). Pareto efficiency means that it is impossible to make any individual better off without making at least one other individual worse off. The theorem holds with selfish preferences, that is, where agents derive utility from just their own consumption of goods. The theorem might be taken to imply that in a properly working market economy, there is no role for altruism; self-interest is sufficient to produce an efficient outcome; this is a conclusion reminiscent of Adam Smith's 'invisible hand', whereby the pursuit of self-interest by all produces a harmonious social optimum. But this conclusion is too hasty; it may be the case that there is no role for altruism to make everybody better off in such an economy, but it is still the case that altruism might be employed to improve the distribution of income, about which the Pareto criterion is silent. (Of course, if lump-sum taxes and transfers are used by the government to bring about an optimal distribution of income, there is no role for altruism for this purpose, either.) But also, it is fairly clear that the world in which we live is nothing like the Walrasian economy which features in the theorem. One could give a long list of divergences; here is a brief and incomplete list: the real world is not perfectly competitive; markets do not always clear; externalities and public goods exist; information is always

imperfect and often asymmetric; the model assumes that production and exchange is the only way of acquiring goods, ruling out theft and giving. What the theorem does perhaps show is that there may be circumstances under which altruism may not be necessary and where the pursuit of self-interest is appropriate and may indeed produce desirable results, but this depends very much on the environment within which this takes place. If there are problems, perhaps because of at least one of the assumptions of the theorem failing to hold, then the appropriate remedy may be to change the environment within which self-interest operates, rather than trying to encourage people to behave in non-selfish ways. An example: suppose a firm pollutes the environment, then the appropriate remedy may be to impose a tax on the pollution, inducing the firm to do in its own interest what is socially optimal, rather than, say, exhorting the firm to act in a socially responsible way which, one might guess, is unlikely to have the desired effect. There may be other social problems for which it may be more difficult to change the environment so as to induce agents to do in their own interest what is socially optimal. In this case, an altruistic solution may be preferable – it may be desirable to allocate the scarce resources of altruism in a society to areas in which it is clearly superior to the alternatives.

Immiserization due to interdependent utility functions
Bernheim and Stark (1988) argue that with interdependent utility functions, increased altruism may be a source of greater misery. If I care more about suffering in the rest of the world, then, if suffering in the rest of the world increases, I am made worse off than I would have been had my caring not increased. However, we can avoid this conclusion if we make social welfare the sum (or at least an increasing function) of individuals' felicities, as argued above. In this case, my increased caring would not affect social welfare unless it affected individuals' consumption bundles (and other things which might enter into their felicity functions); so social welfare would increase if I gave more to charity, with the marginal utility of the recipient being higher than my marginal utility (of the goods transferred), presumably a necessary condition for my giving in the first place.

The samaritan's dilemma (or the economics of the prodigal son)
Suppose I expect to be supported in my old age by an altruistic benefactor; then I have an incentive to consume excessively in my youth. If I consume an extra £1 when young, then, in the absence of any change in transfers, the cost to me is £1$(1 + R)$ worth of consumption in old age, where R is the relevant interest rate. But it is possible that this reduction in future consumption would be such as to induce my benefactor to transfer extra resources to me. In the limiting case where my future consumption is completely guaranteed by the altruistic donor, then the cost of present consumption, in terms of future consumption, is effec-

tively zero. In the less extreme case where the donor offsets only part of the reduction, the cost of present consumption is still reduced, and it is not difficult to see that this may involve an inefficiency; since my current consumption is effectively subsidized, I will have an incentive to consume too much in the present, knowing that I will be taken care of in the future. The problem would not arise if the benefactor could commit to the level of his future transfer when I make my initial consumption decision, but it is not clear what commitment mechanisms exist in practice. One possibility would be for the benefactor to consume excessively himself in the first period so that he is too poor to make the required transfer in the second period. But this, of course, is costly, and other commitment mechanisms can be expected to be costly as well. It seems, then, that this is a way in which altruism, at least at the family level, can make things worse; an interesting topic for further research is that of specifying institutions that will resolve (or at least mitigate) the problem. It can be suggested that government-run social security schemes might perhaps be defended along these lines. For further discussion of these issues, see Bernheim and Stark (1988) and Lindbeck and Weibull (1988).

Altruism and the enforcement of co-operative agreements
Bernheim and Stark (1988) present another way in which altruism may make things worse: suppose there is a co-operative agreement between two parties which is enforced by some sort of mechanism such as reversion to a Nash equilibrium (it may be remembered that we defined a Nash equilibrium above – it occurs when each agent is doing as well as possible for himself, given the behaviour of others). Since the Nash equilibrium may not be a particularly desirable equilibrium (as was shown by the discussion of the prisoner's dilemma), it may be the case that agents seek to improve on it, but this may involve co-operation in a situation where there is an incentive to defect. Altruism may, on the one hand, have the desirable effect of making the parties more willing to co-operate; on the other hand, it may have the adverse effect of reducing the severity of the 'punishment' strategy (reversion to the Nash equilibrium), hence making the co-operative agreement more difficult to sustain. Bernheim and Stark show that, with increased altruism, the second effect might well outweigh the first and so make such agreements more difficult to sustain. An analogy may be useful. Suppose we consider the bad old days of the Cold War, and two countries, the Soviet Union and the United States, both of whom could obliterate the other with nuclear weapons, but without being able to destroy the other country's ability to retaliate. It might be argued that, if a nuclear attack has taken place on one of the countries, it is irrational for that country to retaliate; retaliation will make things even worse for the potential retaliator if it is at all altruistic towards the citizens of the aggressor. If it is indeed the case that an attacked country would have no incentive to retaliate, there is no credible deterrent

effect of nuclear weapons and we might expect a first strike (assume a country would benefit by attacking the other with nuclear weapons if the other does not retaliate). Suppose now we reduce the degree of altruism between the two countries by introducing negative altruism (hatred?), which would be especially prevalent in a country which had just experienced a nuclear attack (assuming some survivors, who would be unlikely to feel particularly well-disposed towards the inhabitants of a country which had just eliminated most of their compatriots). It may not take much hatred to make retaliation in the aftermath of a nuclear attack a rational response, and thus for nuclear weapons to be a credible deterrent (so the desirable co-operative arrangement is sustained). One suspects, though, that mankind would have been better off if there had been less hatred between nations in the course of human history.

Imperfect information and altruism
Above it was argued that altruism may have a role in situations of asymmetric information. However, we can argue that there are situations involving asymmetric information in which altruism may not be such a good idea. Suppose a choice is to be made as to where I am to live, with housing allocated altruistically on the basis of 'need'; then it may not be easy to communicate my 'needs' to the body which allocates the housing, and, in any case, this body will surely have imperfect information about my needs and preferences and may well make an incorrect decision, given available resource constraints. It might seem much better to allow me to make the appropriate choice myself, subject to relevant constraints on how much of society's resources I can use. In many situations this is provided by the price mechanism. So the most efficient way of enabling me to obtain a certain level of well-being may be to allocate me a certain level of income, and to allow me to use it in the way I please to purchase goods. The point is that each person has far more information about his preferences and what contributes to his well-being than anyone else (there are a few qualifications to this which should not concern us) and allowing him or her to make a fair number of decisions (particularly in the areas of consumption choices, career decisions and relationships) in order to satisfy these preferences, might be efficient from society's point of view. Altruism often has additional informational requirements – if I am to benefit another person, I need to know what will benefit him, and it may not be easy to acquire the relevant information. Acting egoistically may not run into these particular problems (it may not be necessary for one person to acquire information about another under an egoistic mechanism, whereas this may be necessary for altruistic action).

It is in this way that I believe it might be possible to give an account of why freedom is valuable, if one adopts the philosophy that what matters is the sum of (or at least an increasing function of) the welfare levels of the individuals in society. Allowing people the freedom to make certain choices which are important from the point of view of their welfare may be the best way of promoting social welfare; restricting freedom may be appropriate when individuals may not be making decisions which are conducive to their own or society's welfare. One reason an individual may make wrong choices is that he lacks the relevant information; however, it does not seem that this necessarily implies that his freedom should be interfered with. A better remedy may be merely to provide the relevant information. Only when this is difficult or impossible would interfering with his liberty seem desirable. An example: suppose I notice someone who is standing, unbeknownst to himself, in the path of an oncoming train. He is obviously lacking information very relevant for his welfare! (Assume I know he is not rationally attempting suicide; readers might consider how the argument should be modified if this is a possibility.) The best thing to do may well be to shout a warning, that is, to provide the relevant information, and to allow him to take the appropriate action himself. There may be circumstances under which it is not possible to communicate the information in time – for example, he may be deaf, or not understand any language I speak. In this case pushing him out of the path of the train – that is, interfering with his liberty – is the right thing to do. I conclude that a promising direction for research on freedom and the circumstances under which interference with freedom (for paternalistic or other reasons) is appropriate concerns the analysis of optimal social institutions in situations where individuals have private information. (Another way in which altruism may make things worse, which is worth a brief mention, is when the intending benefactor makes a mistake, and ends up making things worse. We can probably all think of sincerely proclaimed ethical ideals which end up making things worse; this point is stressed by Samuel Brittan in his contribution to this volume.)

Co-ordination problems

There are some social problems which cannot be ascribed to selfishness and for which altruism is not a solution. One prime example is that of what might be described as co-ordination problems; an example of such a problem is given in Figure 9.5. It is fairly obvious that this game has two equilibria ((R1, C1) and (R2, C2)), the first Pareto dominating the second. Examples of co-ordination problems are not difficult to find: we might mention the choice of a currency or language or the question of which side of the road to drive on. It is fairly clear that there may be many solutions to these problems. It may be contended that what is most important is that people co-ordinate, rather than the precise solution adopted. Yet some solutions to co-ordination problems dominate others and are not chosen. For example, it has been argued that the current layout of the typewriter keyboard is inefficient and could be improved upon; some languages may be very difficult to learn and use and it would be much easier if everyone spoke one easy language such as Esperanto. It can also be shown that altruism will in no way solve the problem; not all societal problems are due to selfishness and can be removed with sufficient altruism.

Column

		C1	C2
	R1	5 , 5	0 , 0
Row			
	R2	0 , 0	4 , 4

Figure 9.5   A co-ordination game

Concluding comments

One further issue we will consider briefly in this final section is that of the implications of the extent to which altruism is exhibited in a society or social grouping. There is an interesting result, known as the rotten-kid theorem (see Becker, 1991, Ch. 8), according to which it is necessary for just one member of a group to behave altruistically (usually the family is the unit in question) to ensure that each member of the group acts in the best interests of the group. The argument is somewhat as follows: call the altruist the father, and suppose he can make lump-sum transfers between the members of the family. Suppose a kid in the family sees a money-making opportunity for himself (he stands to gain £500, say), but this is at the expense of another member of the family, who will lose £700 from such an action. Then undertaking the action might appear to be in the kid's selfish interest, although it is not, of course, in the interest of the family. However, the father will, according to the theorem, reduce his transfer to the kid if he does misbehave by more than £500 and compensate the loser (he might also adjust transfers to other members of the family). It hence will not be in the kid's interest to carry out the action, since he will, on balance, come out a loser. So egoistic members of the family will be induced to do, in their own interest, what is in the best interest of the family. The rotten-kid theorem is neat and has been subject to a fair amount of analysis recently (see, for example, Bergstrom, 1989; Bruce and Waldman, 1990). The following points are relevant:

1. The theorem presupposes that transfers are operative under all circumstances; if a kid reaches a border solution – that is, his transfer goes to zero – the theorem no longer holds.
2. The case where there is more than one altruist has been little analysed, but it seems probable that in these circumstances the theorem would no longer

    hold (there might, for example, be strategic interaction or co-ordination problems among the altruists).

3. The theorem may not hold if the altruist has imperfect information about some of the opportunities or characteristics of the family. For example, suppose a kid has an opportunity to work for £5 per hour and will work (in the absence of changes in transfers) until his marginal disutility of working equals the wage. This would also be in the best interest of the family. But if the father does not know the marginal disutility of working function of the kid, he may effectively tax the earnings of the kid and hence give the kid an incentive to work less. This would seem to be the crucial difficulty with applying the theorem at the societal level – the benevolent donor (the state?) surely has inadequate information to make appropriate transfers.

4. What happens under uncertainty in the rotten-kid case has been little analysed but could be interesting, particularly if in some circumstances a boundary solution is reached. For example, might the kid not have an incentive to buy lottery tickets which give him a small chance of a large gain? If he doesn't win, then he's compensated, but if he wins, assuming his winnings exceed his initial transfer from his father, he is better off. There might be similar problems with career choice (as between a risky and safer career).

It seems, then, that the theorem is subject to a fair number of limitations and we would not expect its conclusion, that all members of a group act in the group's best interest, to be a reasonable description of reality. But that is perhaps not the point; what the theorem does is to provide a benchmark and a key result which any rigorous analysis of the behaviour of families and other social groups needs to take into account. It might perhaps best be described as a theorem about a benevolent dictator, since the altruist needs to have considerable power for the result to hold. Unfortunately, it is difficult to think of any mechanism for ensuring that societies are ruled by benevolent dictators. The theorem also provides an example of how a limited amount of altruism in a society may be sufficient to achieve what is socially optimal.

    A number of directions for research are suggested by the analysis of this chapter. One promising direction seems to be that of analysing the role of altruism in situations of asymmetric information. Analysis of models with asymmetric information has been a fairly active topic of recent research in economic theory and game theory, but few of these models, to my knowledge, have incorporated altruism.[8]

    The role of altruism in the economy is complex, and it is not possible to come to the apparently simple conclusion that a little more altruism would be a good thing. It is certainly true that in certain situations altruism may make things better, but in other circumstances it may make things worse. In certain contexts altruism may make a big difference to the resolution of a social problem (for example, blood donation) even if only a small proportion of the population is altruistic; in other contexts it is probably necessary that the bulk of the population behave in ways which might be described as altruistic if altruism is to have a significant effect.

Notes

1. I am grateful to John Flemming, Alan Hamlin and participants in the British Association Meetings for helpful comments and discussion, but accept full blame for all remaining deficiencies.
2. We would also observe that economic models are often set up in such a way that agents have no opportunity for behaving non-egoistically. For example, in many economic models, consumers are able to choose their own consumption bundle, subject to a budget constraint, but are unable to influence other consumers' choices. In order to analyse altruism in economic models, it is obviously necessary that the models incorporate ways in which altruistic behaviour is at least possible! One possibility is to allow agents to make transfers to others. Other models incorporate the possibility of altruism in different ways; examples include models in which agents can choose the price at which they trade, or where agents can choose the amount (or type) of information to reveal.
3. We would want to include under altruism commitments to unknown individuals (for example, those who have suffered in a natural disaster in a far away land) and also to as yet non-existent members of future generations. One might also include commitments to non-human beings (an example would be vegetarianism, motivated by the belief that it is wrong to kill animals in order to eat them).
4. However, there may be some prisoner's dilemmas where taxation or government intervention cannot be used to resolve the problem. The government may not possess relevant information, or may be unable to tax or penalize the undesirable activity. In such cases, altruism may be particularly important.
5. See Arrow (1972) and Singer (1973).
6. Of course, it would be ridiculous to suggest that the used car market, the archetypal lemons market, be organized on the basis of voluntary donations, which may be appropriate for only a very few commodities, such as blood, with very special characteristics. But it might be suggested that greater honesty on the part of sellers in the market would be desirable.
7. Possible examples might be two friends who come to blows in a restaurant, each insisting on paying for the other's meal, and two excessively polite people each of whom insists that the other enters a room first.
8. One area of economics in which models with altruism have been employed extensively is in the analysis of the circumstances under which Ricardian equivalence holds (that is, the view that the time pattern of taxes used to finance a given sequence of public expenditures is irrelevant, which means that government budget deficits – if caused by tax changes – have no economic effects). These models have not been discussed in this chapter, but have been accorded ample space in the literature – for a survey see Bernheim (1987).

Bibliography

Akerlof, G. (1970), 'The Market for Lemons: Qualitative Uncertainty and the Market Mechanism', *Quarterly Journal of Economics*, **84**, 488–500.

Andreoni, J. (1989), 'Giving with Impure Altruism: Applications to Charity and Ricardian Equivalence', *Journal of Political Economy*, **97**, 1447–58.

Arrow, K. (1972), 'Gifts and Exchanges', *Philosophy and Public Affairs*, **1**, 343–62.

Arrow, K. (1984), 'Optimal and Voluntary Income Distribution', in *Collected Papers of Kenneth J. Arrow: Volume 1, Social Choice and Justice*, Oxford: Basil Blackwell.

Becker, G. (1991), *A Treatise on the Family*, enlarged edition, Cambridge: Harvard University Press.

Bergstrom, T. (1989), 'A Fresh Look at the Rotten Kid Theorem – and Other Household Mysteries', *Journal of Political Economy*, **97**, 1138–59.

Bergstrom, T. and Stark, O. (1993), 'How Altruism can Prevail in an Evolutionary Environment', *American Economic Review, Papers and Proceedings*, **83**, 149–55.

Bernheim, D. (1987), 'Ricardian Equivalence: An Evaluation of Theory and Evidence', *NBER Macroeconomics Annual*.

Bernheim, D. and Stark, O. (1988), 'Altruism within the Family Reconsidered: Do Nice Guys Finish Last?', *American Economic Review*, **78**, 1034–45.

Blackorby, C. and Donaldson, D. (1992), 'Pigs and Guinea Pigs: A Note on the Ethics of Animal Exploitation', *Economic Journal*, **102**, 1345–69.

Broome, J. (1992), *Counting the Cost of Global Warming*, Cambridge: White Horse Press.

Bruce, N. and Waldman, M. (1990), 'The Rotten-Kid Theorem Meets the Samaritan's Dilemma', *Quarterly Journal of Economics*, **105**, 155–66.

Collard, D. (1978), *Altruism and Economy*, Oxford: Martin Robertson.

Hammond, P. (1987), 'Altruism', in Eatwell, J., Milgate, M. and Newman, P. (eds), *The New Palgrave: A Dictionary of Economics*, Basingstoke: Macmillan.

Hausman, D. and McPherson, M. (1993), 'Taking Ethics Seriously: Economics and Contemporary Moral Philosophy', *Journal of Economic Literature*, **31**, 671–731.

Kolm, S.C. (1983), 'Altruism', *Ethics*, **94**, 18–65.

Kotlikoff, L., Razin, A. and Rosenthal, R. (1990), 'A Strategic Altruism Model in which Ricardian Equivalence Does Not Hold', *Economic Journal*, **100**, 1261–8.

Kranich, L. (1988), 'Altruism and Efficiency: A Welfare Analysis of the Walrasian Mechanism with Transfers', *Journal of Public Economics*, **36**, 369–86.

Kreps, D. (1990), A Course in Microeconomic Theory, Princeton: Princeton University Press.

Kurz, M. (1977), 'Altruistic Equilibrium', in Balassa, B. and Nelson, R. (eds), *Economic Progress, Private Values and Public Policy*, Amsterdam: North-Holland.

Lindbeck, A. and Weibull, J. (1988), 'Altruism and Time Consistency: The Economics of Fait Accompli', *Journal of Political Economy*, **96**, 1165–82.

Mansbridge, J. (1990), *Beyond Self-Interest*, Chicago: University of Chicago Press.

Monroe, K., Barton, M. and Klingemann, U. (1990), 'Altruism and the Theory of Rational Action: Rescuers of Jews in Nazi Europe', *Ethics*, **101**, 103–22.

Parfit, D. (1984), *Reasons and Persons*, Oxford: Clarendon Press.

Paul, E., Miller, F. and Paul, J. (1993), *Altruism*, Cambridge: Cambridge University Press.

Phelps, E. (1975), (ed.), *Altruism, Morality and Economic Theory*, New York: Russell Sage Foundation.

Samuelson, P. (1993), 'Altruism as a Problem Involving Group versus Individual Selection in Economics and Biology', *American Economic Review*, **83**, 143–8.

Sen, A. (1990), 'Rational Fools: A Critique of the Behavioural Foundations of Economic Theory', in Mansbridge, J. (ed.), *Beyond Self-Interest*, Chicago: University of Chicago Press.

Simon, H. (1993), 'Altruism and Economics', *American Economic Review, Papers and Proceedings*, **83**, 156–61.

Singer, P. (1973), 'Altruism and Commerce: A defense of Titmuss Against Arrow', *Philosophy and Public Affairs*, **2**, 312–20.

Stark, O. (1989), 'Altruism and the Quality of Life', *American Economic Review, Papers and Proceedings*, **79**, 86–90.

Sugden, R. (1982), 'On the Economics of Philanthropy', *Economic Journal*, **92**, 341–58.

Titmuss, R. (1970), *The Gift Relationship*, London: Allen and Unwin.

10 The moral of the market
Alan Hamlin

Introduction

Although it is only a subset of the debate on the links between ethics and economics, the debate on the relationship between market capitalism and moral values is complex and multi-dimensional. The various essays collected here pursue lines of inquiry which focus on different aspects of this relationship and which utilize different styles of analysis. While this variety reflects the richness of the debate in the area, it can leave the reader unsure of the connections between the various arguments deployed, and of the place of individual arguments in the overall debate. The major purpose of this chapter is, therefore, to offer an overview of the debate as a whole within which these particular arguments can be set.

How might the relationship between market capitalism and morality be analysed? Without any claim to either originality or completeness, it is useful to identify three aspects of this relationship:[1]

1. Market capitalism might itself depend upon the satisfaction of moral background conditions and, in particular, on the moral beliefs and views of individual agents. We might term this the moral *basis* of markets. The potential problems here include the possibility of incompatibility between the moral character of individual agents required to satisfy the background conditions for markets to exist, and the character of agents required to operate efficient markets. A second potential problem derives from the possibility that the operation of market capitalism might causally influence the moral beliefs and views of individual agents, so that the moral background conditions may be eroded over time.

2. Moral considerations might also arise in determining the range of application of market capitalism – that is, in determining which aspects of society should, and should not, be allocated to the 'market sphere'.[2] We might term this the moral *scope* of markets. Problems arising in this area include the substantive questions of whether this or that activity should be mediated through the market, and the more formal question of how the moral limits of the market sphere might be determined in principle.

3. Even within the market sphere, a further set of moral questions arises concerning the normative assessment of market processes and outcomes themselves. We might term this the moral *evaluation* of markets. Problems

arising in this area include the normative questions associated with inequality and poverty in market economies, and the moral arguments for intervention in market processes or outcomes.

Of course, these three aspects of the relationship between morality and markets interact with one another. It should, for example, be obvious that any discussion of the moral scope of the market must depend to some extent on the views taken about the moral evaluation of the market. Nevertheless, I would claim that the distinctions between these three aspects are sufficiently clear for them to provide a useful starting point. The main body of this chapter will be structured to discuss each of these aspects in turn. But first it is appropriate to identify some general concerns with the application of moral arguments at the institutional level, and sketch the general lines along which normative arguments in support of the market are constructed.

Morality and institutions

Before delving into the morality of the market in more detail it is worthwhile pausing to consider the nature of that inquiry. In particular we might ask, is the market as an institution the sort of thing which can be the subject of moral inquiry? Some would argue that the only proper subjects for moral inquiry are moral agents rather than institutional structures. Thus, the character and actions of individuals may be considered from the moral standpoint, but not the circumstances in which these individuals act. This seems clear where the circumstances are themselves entirely outside of control – as might be the case with the climate. Here we might agree that it would be meaningless to speak of the morality of rainfall, or of a hurricane. But where the circumstances are social rather than physical or natural, the argument seems less clear.

Hayek (1960) suggests that it is no more sensible to discuss the morality of the market as an institution than it is to discuss the morality of the climate. The basis of this argument is that the outcomes of the market are not directly chosen or intended by any individual – but are rather the unintended outcome of a myriad of separate and independent decisions mediated through the institution of the market. This argument seems to take the market as a simple social fact – just as the climate might be taken as a simple natural fact – beyond the control of agents. However, the idea of discussing the morality of the market seems to be predicated on the idea that the market is not beyond our control, but that we can, at least to some extent, influence the institutional structure in which we operate. Of course, such influence must be exercised within the constraints of feasibility – and much of Hayek's argument can be read as a warning against the dangers of Utopian social planning of all types – but these constraints leave some discretion and it is here that the questions of morality must be relevant.

This leads to a secondary issue. If the market is a proper subject for moral inquiry, how should that inquiry be conducted? In particular, it is clear that social outcomes will depend partly on the characteristics of social institutions and partly on the characteristics of the individuals operating within those institutions. If we are to inquire about the morality of the institutions, what should we assume about the characters of the individuals? Four possibilities seem particularly salient. First, we might assume that individuals are themselves moral, so that we focus on the possibility that institutional failings might subvert the morality of society.[3] Secondly, we might assume that individuals are immoral, so that we focus on the possibility of institutions rescuing society from immorality. Thirdly, we might assume that individuals are amoral, so that we focus on the moral properties induced by institutions against a morally neutral background. Fourthly, we might attempt to model individuals as they actually are, a complex and heterogeneous mix of morality and immorality, so as to focus on predicting the actual outcomes of any particular institutional arrangement.

Each of these approaches has its merits, and it might be particularly interesting to view institutions under a variety of assumptions about individual moral character, but to the economist the two major alternatives must be the third and fourth. The assumption that each individual is a prudent but essentially amoral maximizer of his or her own utility is not descriptively accurate. But, as Bertrand Russell (quoted by Samuel Brittan on p. 3) reminds us, neither is self-interest the most pessimistic assumption. The choice between descriptive accuracy and the moderate pessimism and moral neutrality of assuming individuals to be amoral must be made on methodological grounds.

Brennan and Buchanan (1983) argue that, even if we had available to us a descriptively accurate model of the moral character of individuals, we should use the more pessimistic, amoral, model when analysing alternative institutional frameworks with a view to institutional or constitutional reform. The argument is essentially that institutions form a sort of insurance – that they should be robust against minor variations in the character of individuals and should perform reasonably even when individuals do not. This is the basic insight contained in the frequently quoted remark of David Hume's that:

> in constraining any system of government, and fixing the several checks and controls of the constitution, every man ought to be supposed a knave, and to have no other end, in all his actions, than private interest (Hume, 1985, p. 42).

Although this argument was originally aimed at the design of political institutions, it applies with equal force to social institutions in general.

A second point concerns the moral neutrality of the assumption of self-interest. This relates to the basic structure of 'invisible hand' arguments in which desired outcomes are generated by the institutional structure – that is, the pattern and form of relationships between agents – rather than by direct appeal to the motivations of the agents themselves. The choice of the assumption of amoral agents then focuses attention on the search for invisible hand mechanisms – mechanisms which economize on virtue in the sense that they do not require virtuous agents.

This is important both because of the special power of invisible hand arguments and because of the limitations of such arguments. For example, one type of social institution which will not appear to be effective under the assumption of amoral agents, but which may work in practice, is the type of institution which seeks to screen out the more moral members of a society, or socialize certain individuals to particular moral standards, in order to place them in certain significant roles. The 'public service tradition' so evident in the British civil service in the late 19th and early 20th century might be an example of an attempt to socialize individuals into a particular outlook, while the method of selecting and rewarding judges (usually involving a significant reduction in salary) might provide an example of a screening process. Such institutions are not invisible hand mechanisms since they depend on the existence of 'more moral members' of society. The aim with this type of institution is to amplify the social effects of existing moral character, and if this is the type of institution of interest, it would be more appropriate to base analysis on a plausibly realistic view of moral character.

In short, there is a role for both the amoral assumption and for greater descriptive realism. Each approach focuses on a different type of institutional effect – the invisible hand case and the 'amplification' case. Excessive reliance on either approach may divert attention from the variety of ways in which institutions may operate to influence outcomes for better or for worse.

Normative support for the market

The market is an institutional structure for decentralized decision-making on the questions of what is to be produced, by what method, by whom and for whom. As normally conceived, the market system is not an all-enveloping social institution, but is embedded within a wider set of institutions which together characterize a society. Some of these institutions have relatively clear structures – such as the law – while others are more amorphous in nature – such as the social customs and norms which provide the context for many social interactions. It is this simple fact that the market is one social institution among many that points to the importance of the question of the moral *scope* of markets.

Normative arguments in support of a relatively wide-ranging and free market system come in a wide variety of forms. It is useful to identify three key ingredients which arise in differing combinations in many of these arguments: an efficiency ingredient, a procedural ingredient and a feasibility ingredient.

The efficiency ingredient focuses on the outcomes of free markets and, in its most powerful form, argues that the outcome of utility-maximizing behaviour in the context of a full set of competitive markets is efficient in the Paretian sense. This is the fundamental theorem of welfare economics discussed by John Fender (pp. 128–9), which may be thought of as a formalization of Adam Smith's claim concerning the invisible hand property of the market mechanism. Nigel Lawson (p. 43) also clearly refers to this line of argument in pointing to the productive power of the market capitalist system. A point to notice here is that the fundamental welfare theorem depends on the assumption of rational and own-utility maximizing individuals just as much as it depends on a full set of competitive markets.

The procedural ingredient to the arguments in support of markets picks up on two clear moral values – autonomy and liberty. Autonomy, in this setting, might be construed as indicating the ability of individuals to determine their own life-plans and their own ends, while liberty might be construed as indicating the ability of individuals to act in accordance with their own plans with a minimum of interference. The market is then claimed to offer an environment which is particularly supportive of both autonomy and liberty-autonomy to the extent that the market recognizes each individual's preferences as sovereign, so that there is no paternalistic determination of ends, and liberty to the extent that the voluntary actions involved in trading reflect the absence of coercion. Amartya Sen (pp. 25–6 and 1985a) and Nigel Lawson refer to these arguments deriving from the voluntary nature of market activity.[4]

The feasibility ingredient switches the focus of attention away from substantive moral claims concerning either the market mechanism or its expected outcomes and towards the constraints imposed on any decision-making procedure faced with the challenge of the key economic questions – what to produce, how to produce it, by whom and for whom. The key constraint in this context is often seen – following Hayek (1937, 1945) – as informational. The point here is that any decision-making system must take account of the radically distributed nature of information about technology, talents and tastes; so that the key attribute of any system must be its ability to operate in such an informational environment, and to provide mechanisms which reveal relevant information. The market is seen as uniquely capable in this respect.

The moral basis of the market

I have already noted that the market can only be seen as one institution among many, embedded within society and supported by a wide range of other institutions. The first question to arise in this context is: are the background requirements of the market model inconsistent with the motivational assumptions within the market model? In other words, are supporters of the market in the position of having to take individuals as selfish maximizers within the market, but trusting moral agents in the social background to the market? It is this question that occupies much of the discussion in the chapters by Samuel Brittan, Amartya Sen and Norman Barry, and also relates to the discussion offered by Nigel Lawson and John Fender.

I would like to provide a background to their discussion by identifying two possible strategies for resolving any apparent tension between the foreground assumption of self-interested rationality and the background assumption of moral agency. The first strategy is to argue that the background morality is, on further analysis, consistent with the foreground model of self-interest; while the second strategy is to argue that the foreground model of self-interest is inessential and that the market can be supported in a way which is directly consistent with the background model of morality. These two strategies differ dramatically in that the first attempts to analyse all institutions in terms of (enlightened) self-interest, while the second attempts to defend the market in directly moral terms by departing from the assumption of amoral self-interest. The first strategy can therefore be identified with the approach which seeks to find invisible hand mechanisms at work in a wide range of social institutions, while the second can be identified with the alternative approach to institutions grounded in moral agency.

The first strategy seeks to ground trust and other apparently moral aspects of background behaviour in rational self-interest. The basic idea here – discussed by Samuel Brittan and John Fender – is that in repeated interactions it will often be rational to act as if you are following a moral code such as 'always keep your promises', because the long-term pay-off to promise-keeping is greater than the long-term pay-off to promise-breaking once you account for the impact of promise-breaking on the future (that is, your future promises will not be believed). In this way honesty, and other apparently moral behaviour patterns, is often the best policy, and conventions of honesty might be expected to arise and endure.

Such conventions are fundamentally self-enforcing, even in a society of rational and self-interested individuals. And it is at least possible that the stock of self-enforcing conventions and norms is sufficiently rich to support market institutions – that is, to provide the relatively rich set of background institutions, ranging from property rights to conventions of trust and co-operation.[5]

The second argument takes the opposite tack of admitting moral character which goes well beyond rational self-interest and attempting to resolve the tension between the market and the social background in this way. But notice a problem here: if we move away from the assumption of self-interested rationality, we no longer have direct access to the fundamental welfare theorem in support of market institutions. If individuals are motivated in some more moral manner – perhaps with some degree of altruism as discussed by John Fender – it is relatively easy to construct cases in which voluntary trade between such apparently moral individuals leads to Pareto-inefficient outcomes. If rational egoists can be led as if by an invisible hand to serve the general interest, so more moral individuals can be tripped by an invisible foot in their attempts to serve the general interest.

Of course, this problem need not be fatal. It may be that in at least some cases a version of the fundamental welfare theorem can be proved for motivations which ascribe more complex moral characters to individuals. Or, even if a degree of efficiency is sacrificed, there are still the procedural and feasibility arguments available for the defence of market institutions.

The point here is not to favour one strategy over the other, but simply to identify them as distinct approaches and to recognize their implications. If the first strategy is adopted, the implied research agenda involves the study of the limits of rational self-interest and the connections between rationality and morality;[6] while if the second strategy is adopted, the focus of attention must be on modelling the moral character of individuals and assessing the implications for the analysis of markets.

A second major question arising in the area of the moral basis of the market is the question of the possible endogeneity of preferences or, more generally, moral character. It might be argued that market institutions actually encourage the pursuit of self-interest, so that constant exposure to market pressures results in a form of moral desensitization – we become slaves to the market, and the social fabric that supported the market is eaten away. The argument here is essentially a form of negative feedback – we start out with moral characters which support the background institutions of society which in turn support the market, but the use of the market progressively shifts our moral perspective in the direction of self-interest. In the short term this might be expected to lead to increased use of the market as an institution (and the decline of non-market institutions) as self-interest comes to dominate; but, taken to the limit, this shift towards self-interest might undermine the background conditions essential to the market, so that the market would fail in its own terms.

Extending this line of speculation might suggest that as the market fails, moral perspectives might shift back away from self-interest, alternative institutions might be expected to replace the market, and the social fabric might re-emerge, so that the cycle could begin again.[7]

The moral scope of the market

The central question in the debate on the *scope* of the market is one of balance rather than of simple choice. Few – if any – would deny that the market is an appropriate institution for the conduct of some aspects of social life; few – if any – would argue that the market is the only institution required for successful or satisfactory social life. The question is one of the appropriate balance between market and non-market institutions and the appropriate allocation of aspects of social life as between the various institutions.

I do not intend to attempt to identify the appropriate scope of the market in practical terms – where in the range from standard commodities such as chocolate bars and television sets to items such as human organs and the survival of a species of animal, the line between the marketable and the non-marketable should be drawn. Rather I shall be content to sketch a line of argument that might lead in the right direction, and which illustrates some of the key ideas in this debate.

Start from the presumption that there are many different values which may be affirmed by a rational agent – happiness, friendship, autonomy, fairness and so on. The standard economist – and many others, including many philosophers – would argue that all of these values are commensurable and may be reduced to a single underlying scale of value. This is a contentious matter, but grant this commensurability for the moment.[8]

A basic question, then, concerns the relationships between these various values and their implications for social and institutional arrangements. One view – which might be thought of as the extreme limit of the standard economist's view – is that since all values are commensurable, we may label the underlying scale of value as 'utility' and proceed on this basis to defend the market as the institutional setting which will best promote the utility of all agents. This would seem to imply that everything should be marketable and that all relationships between agents should be contractual. Many might think this a form of economic brutalism.

A second view – which might be thought of as being at the opposite extreme – rejects commensurability and insists that different values require different institutional settings for their promotion and realization. Thus, in this view, the market should be limited to those areas concerned with the promotion or realization of certain values – particularly the self-interested values associated with simple preference satisfaction – and other institutional arrangements utilized in pursuit of other values. Perhaps political institutions, or the institutions of family or community, might be appropriate where the market is seen as inappropriate. Furthermore, since this view rejects commensurability, there can be no argument of the form that one value is more important than another; each value – and the entailed institutional arrangement – can only be promoted in its own terms.

While this argument may be extreme, is does contain a basic and powerful insight – that institutional arrangements are not neutral with respect to values. But this insight might be accommodated within a more moderate argument which retains the commitment to commensurability.

Suppose that all values are indeed commensurable – so that we may speak of balancing one value against another and reaching all-things-considered judgements. But suppose also that there are links between values and institutional arrangements. Some values – we might term them efficiency for convenience – might be particularly associated with the institution of the market; other values might be particularly associated with other institutions. To pick up on John Broome's discussion, the value of fairness might be particularly associated with institutions such as lotteries which treat all claims equally. If all this is true, then selecting between institutional arrangements might be conceived as a matter of choosing the value-maximizing institution, while recognizing the structural link between certain values and certain institutions.

Thus, if fairness is particularly important to us in some specific context, (as it might be in the allocation of organs for transplant) we might choose a lottery-type institution, but choose it on the grounds that it maximizes all-things-considered value. This may seem odd. John Broome is at pains to contrast the claim of fairness with the claim of doing the most good,[9] and yet I am suggesting that we might choose the lottery mechanism precisely on the grounds that it does the most good. But this difficulty is removed once it is recognized that fairness itself contributes to the good, so that acting fairly in this context substitutes one sort of good (fairness) for another (choosing the patient so as to maximize the direct benefit to the treated patient); and it is at least reasonable to suggest that it should be done only if, all things considered, good is increased. Surely, we would not wish to implement a fair allocation mechanism *whatever* the cost.

The key to this type of argument is the commensurability of values and the construction of all-things-considered rankings of alternatives. In switching from one institutional regime to another, each type of value may react differently – in our example the expected direct benefits of treatment will decrease and the fairness will increase as we shift to a lottery system – but so long as values are commensurable we can always ask the further question of which regime best promotes value overall. Only when values are held to be strongly incommensurable is this question unanswerable in principle.

This line of argument suggests that it might be possible to delimit the scope of the market, and of any other institution, by reference to all-things-considered judgements about alternative institutional regimes, where those judgements are sensitive to the links between values and institutions. It might be worth stressing that this argument attempts to combine a form of value-pluralism with an underlying commensurability of values. This is achieved by rejecting the idea that all values are simply reducible to some simple substantive value – for example, pleasure – while accepting that the many distinct values can be compared by use of a common scale of value. Of course, if commensurability is rejected, so that values are not only distinct but also incomparable, this line of argument fails.

The moral evaluation of markets

As we have just seen, addressing questions about the moral scope of an institution will require positions to be taken on some of the fundamental questions which arise in attempting to evaluate that institution. Are institutions to be judged by their expected consequences, or by the degree to which they respect rights or other constraints? If by their consequences, which consequences and how should they be valued? If by the respect for deontic constraints, which constraints apply and with what force? These are among the grand themes of ethical debate.

The more specific debate over the moral evaluation of markets can usefully be split into two parts. On the one hand we have the debate in which participants agree – more or less – on the operating characteristics of the market process, but disagree on the relevant ethical criterion. On the other hand we have the debate in which participants agree – more or less – on the ethical criterion, but disagree on the analysis of the characteristics of the market process. Examples of both of these debates can be found in this volume.

On the one hand Nigel Lawson, J.M. Keynes – as represented by Robert Skidelsky – and John Broome can be seen to be engaged in a debate on the appropriate ethical criterion to apply. Leaving aside the differences that these three have on matters to do with the analysis of the market process, Nigel Lawson can be seen as arguing for a moral criterion based essentially on preference satisfaction and autonomy – a form of liberal utilitarianism if you will. J.M. Keynes is clearly portrayed as an ideal utilitarian after G.E. Moore, placing less emphasis on the satisfaction of individual preferences and more emphasis on the achievement of particular ideals of, for example, beauty which are held to be simply good in themselves. By contrast to both of these positions, John Broome argues that, for at least a class of decision-making problems, a relevant criterion is fairness – interpreted not as equality of outcome but as a form of equality of opportunity in which individuals have an appropriate chance of having their claim met.

On the other hand, if we hold constant the moral criterion, we might reasonably interpret some of the discussions offered by John Flemming, and Massimo Beber and Lorenzo Ornaghi, as debates about the practical operation of market institutions in a variety of situations – both dissenting from the extreme view in which markets are held to be rapidly adjusting and continuously equilibrating mechanisms. John Flemming is particularly concerned with the impact of unemployment – particularly as a part of the process of transition to a market economy in Eastern Europe. One part of his concern is that the too rapid adoption of market institutions might threaten social stability, so a slower and more managed transition might be preferred. This same concern would also support intervention of a variety of forms, even in a mature market economy. In one sense, John Flemming paints a version of the traditional picture in which the market is regulated by the political authority, and points to some of the difficulties that can be expected to arise when both the structure of the political authority and the structure of the economy are in flux. Massimo Beber and Lorenzo Ornaghi emphasize the growing dislocation between the institutions of the economy – which they characterize as increasingly global – and the political institutions which attempt to regulate the economy – which still operate mainly at the level of the nation state. Again, the picture is one in which market institutions can be argued to be out of control and capable of generating starkly undesirable outcomes.

In the last section I sketched an overview of the debate on the appropriate scope of the market as an institution, in the remainder of this section it is appropriate to sketch a similar overview of the debate on morally motivated intervention in market mechanisms and their outcomes. I say 'morally motivated' interventions to distinguish two cases. In the first case the practical market is identified as departing from the standard textbook market in some particular regard, and an intervention is proposed to improve the market in its own terms. Thus, for example, we might regard anti-monopoly policy as an example of intervention designed to improve the market. In the second case, the intervention is seen not so much as improving the market in its own terms, but as overriding some aspect of the market. A clear example here is the use of taxes and benefits to override the distribution of income that would arise in the market.

This distinction is important because it separates those interventions which we might think of as being contingent on some particular imperfection in the market as it exists in some place and time, from those interventions which are more principled in the sense that they are motivated by a moral criticism of the market even in its perfect form. It is here that we may return to the three classic ingredients of normative arguments in support of the market – the efficiency ingredient, the procedural ingredient and the feasibility ingredient – and add to this list the classic ingredients of normative arguments in support of intervention in markets.

The first and most important item on this list builds on the distinction between efficiency and good discussed by John Broome. Pareto-efficiency and the good are strongly related only under very particular theories of the good. Thus, for example, if good consists entirely in the satisfaction of actual personal preferences, and if good is interpersonally incomparable, there will be a strong connection between an efficient outcome and a good outcome. But this theory of the good is clearly open to many criticisms.[10] Perhaps the most common line of criticism is that simple preference satisfaction theories of the good, and the notion of efficiency, take no real account of ideas of the satisfaction of needs, rights or considerations of fairness and equity.

I have already suggested that at least some progress may be made in incorporating these and similar ideas into a pluralist but nevertheless commensurable account of value. I will say no more on this here, save to point to this area as a major area of debate in the discussion of the morality of the market.

The second item on the list relates to the procedural ingredient of arguments in support of markets – and is essentially the claim that while the idealized market may promote the procedural values of autonomy and liberty, it may simultaneously deny other procedural values. Clearly if we think of all values – whether procedural or outcome-based – in terms of commensurable values, this point is merged into the first point concerning the nature of good relative to the nature of efficiency. But if these procedural values are intended to have deontic force – as is often the case with claims of rights to liberty, for example – then the point stands separately.

Effectively the point hinges on the appropriate identification of deontic principles – just as the pro-market argument might be associated with affirming commitments to negative liberty and personal autonomy, so the interventionist argument might be associated with affirming commitments to positive liberties, and social solidarity.

The structure of these debates on the free market versus intervention should be clear – whether they are conducted in the language of consequentialist ethics and appeals to the good, or deontic ethics and appeals to the right.[11] This brings me to my final point – the requirement of feasibility. Much of the debate on the morality of markets, market intervention and the alternatives to the market, focuses on the central question of the desirability of alternative structures, while pushing the question of feasibility into the background.[12] But this can often lead to unsatisfactory results. It is all too clear that real-world markets are, at best, very imperfect institutions. The failings of markets are all around us. In some cases, there is even relatively widespread agreement on the general structure of desired interventions – basic income support programmes, a degree of social insurance and so on. But the real debates start with the details.

One particular point that should be stressed is that if markets are to be subject to intervention, the institutions responsible for that intervention – typically the institutions of government – should be subject to the same degree of moral scrutiny as the market. There can be no simple assumption that the regulatory institutions are themselves perfect instruments for the advancement of good. A proper discussion of the appropriate institutional framework for society must place all institutional structures under the analytic lens. The public choice approach to the economics of political institutions and constitutions within the framework normally devoted to the study of the market, provides one basis for making reasonable comparisons across alternative institutional structures.[13]

Economists have often been guilty of analysing markets and market intervention within very crude ethical frameworks, while philosophers have been guilty of failing to engage with the detailed structural and feasibility questions when diagnosing moral problems with the market. The renewed interest among economists and philosophers (and others) in meaningful and productive dialogue between disciplines which has been apparent in recent years holds the promise of real progress on the outstanding questions which still surround the morality of the market.

Notes
1. This categorization might be thought of as a more detailed view of just one part of the categorization of the relationship between ethics and economics offered by Hausman and McPherson (1993) and discussed in Samuel Brittan's chapter of this volume.
2. This usage of 'market sphere' echoes the usage of Walzer (1983) and Anderson (1990, 1993).
3. When the voting procedure advocated by Jean-Charles de Borda was criticized on the grounds that it set up incentives for strategic voting and manipulation, Borda responded that, 'my scheme is only intended for honest men' (quoted in Black, 1958, p. 152). Some might think this an inadequate response.
4. But there are counter-arguments to the effect that in actual market circumstances – rather than idealized market circumstances – market exchange may not be free in the relevant sense, so that markets may themselves be instruments of coercion. See Hobson (1933) and Gibbard (1985).
5. This line of argument is explored further in Hamlin (1986); for an example of a piece of analysis adopting this strategy in attempting to explain the emergence of specific market institutions, see Milgrom, North and Weingast (1990).
6. See, for example, Sugden (1986), Gauthier (1986) and Hardin (1988).
7. A cycle of this general type – between private interests and public actions – is discussed by Hirschman (1982).
8. For discussion see Griffin (1986), for a detailed claim of incommensurability see Anderson (1990, 1993).
9. John Broome also, correctly, distinguishes between doing the most good and acting efficiently in the manner of a perfect market, but this distinction is not crucial here.
10. Some lines of criticism are explored and further references provided in Hamlin (1993).
11. See Miller (1989a, 1989b) and Plant (1989, 1992) for arguments combining a number of these styles of argument.
12. For further discussion of the distinction between desirability and feasibility approaches see Hamlin and Pettit (1989).
13. See, for example, Hamlin (1986) and Brennan and Buchanan (1985).

Bibliography
Anderson, E. (1990), 'The Ethical Limitations of the Market', *Economics and Philosophy*, **6**, 179–205.
Anderson, E. (1993), *Value in Ethics and Economics*, Cambridge: Harvard University Press.
Black, D. (1958), *The Theory of Committees and Elections*, Cambridge: Cambridge University Press.
Brennan, G. and Buchanan, J.M. (1983), 'Predictive Power and the Choice Among Regimes', *Economic Journal*, **93**, 89–105.
Brennan, G. and Buchanan, J.M. (1985), *The Reason of Rules*, Cambridge: Cambridge University Press.
Elster, J. (1986), 'The Market and the Forum', in Elster, J. and Hylland, A. (eds), *Foundations of Social Choice Theory*, Cambridge: Cambridge University Press.
Gauthier, D. (1986), *Morals by Agreement*, Oxford: Oxford University Press.
Gibbard, A. (1985), 'What's Morally Special about Free Exchange?', in Paul, E., Miller, F. and Paul, J. (eds), *Ethics and Economics*, Oxford: Blackwell.
Griffin, J. (1986), *Well-Being: Its Meaning, Measurement and Moral Importance*, Oxford: Oxford University Press.
Hamlin, A. (1986), *Ethics, Economics and the State*, New York: St Martin's Press.
Hamlin, A. (1993), 'Welfare', in Goodin, R. and Pettit, P. (eds), *A Companion to Contemporary Political Philosophy*, Oxford: Blackwell.
Hamlin, A. and Pettit, P. (1989), 'The Normative Analysis of the State', in Hamlin, A. and Pettit, P. (eds), *The Good Polity*, Oxford: Blackwell.
Hardin, R. (1988), *Morality within the Limits of Reason*, Chicago: Chicago University Press.
Hausman, D. and McPherson, M. (1993), 'Taking Ethics Seriously: Economics and Contemporary Moral Philosophy', *Journal of Economic Literature*, **31**, 671–731.
Hayek, F.A. von (1937), 'Economics and Knowledge', *Economica*, **4**, 33–54.

Hayek, F.A. von (1945), 'The Use of Knowledge in Society', *American Economic Review*, 35, 519–30.
Hayek, F.A. von (1960), *The Constitution of Liberty*, London: Routledge.
Hirschman, A. (1982), *Shifting Involvements*, Oxford: Basil Blackwell.
Hobson, J.A. (1933), *The Moral Challenge to the Economic System*, London: The Ethical Union.
Hume, D. (1985), *Essays Moral Political and Literary*, edited by E.F. Miller, Indianapolis: Liberty Classics.
Milgrom, P., North, D. and Weingast, B. (1990), 'The Role of Institutions in the Revival of Trade: The Law Merchant, Private Judges and the Champagne Fairs', *Economics and Politics*, 2, 1–23.
Miller, D. (1989a), *Market State and Community*, Oxford: Oxford University Press.
Miller, D. (1989b), 'Why Markets?', in Le Grand, J. and Estrin, S. (eds), *Market Socialism*, Oxford: Oxford University Press.
Plant, R. (1989), 'Socialism, Markets and End States', in Le Grand, J. and Estrin, S. (eds), *Market Socialism*, Oxford: Oxford University Press.
Plant, R. (1992), 'Enterprise in its Place: The Moral Limits of the Market', in Heelas, P. and Morris, P. (eds), *The Values of the Enterprise Culture*, London: Routledge.
Sen, A.K. (1985a), 'Well-being, Agency and Freedom', *Journal of Philosophy*, 82, 169–221.
Sen, A.K. (1985b), 'The Moral Standing of the Market', in Paul, E., Miller, F. and Paul, J. (eds), *Ethics and Economics*, Oxford: Blackwell.
Sugden, R. (1986), *The Economics of Rights, Cooperation and Welfare*, Oxford: Basil Blackwell.
Walzer, M. (1983), *Spheres of Justice*, New York: Basic Books.

Index

Akerlof, G. 125, 135
Alatas, S. 34
altruism 9, 12–14, 37–8, 46, 57, 66, 94, 102, 117, 120–36, 142
   altruists dilemma 127–9
Anderson, E. 149
Andreoni, J. 135
Aoki, M. 27, 34
Aquinas, T. 106
Aristotle 4, 57, 92, 105
Arrow, K. 107, 118, 135
asymmetric information 125–7, 131–2
Axelrod, R. 11–12, 21

Baker, R. 87
Bannock, G. 71, 78
Barry, N. 78
Barton, M. 136
Beardsley, T. 21
Beauchamp, T. 57, 78
Beber, M. 146
Becker, G. 133, 135
Bentham, J. 93–4, 98
Bergstrom, T. 133, 135, 136
Bernheim, D. 122, 129, 130, 135, 136
Black, D. 149
Blackorby, C. 136
blood donation 8, 14–15, 125–7, 135
Boeing Corporation 73–5
Boesky, I. 58
Borda, C. de. 149
border taxes 52
Bowie, N. 57, 60, 78
Brennan, G. 139, 149
bribery 4–5, 53
Brittan, S. 21, 118, 132, 149
Broome, J. 87, 136, 145, 146, 149
Bruce, N. 133, 136
Buchanan, J. 139, 149
Burke, E. 92–3, 96–8, 100
business ethics 3–4, 16–18, 28–9, 57–78

Cantona, E. 40
Carlyle, T. 6

central planning 51–5
China 3, 36
Coase, R. 66, 78
Collard, D. 136
command economy 4–5, 36
commensurability of values 144–5
commitment 121–3
competition 6, 48, 60–63, 107–9, 111–14, 141
Confucian ethics 27
conventions 2, 16, 48, 142
   see also customs, norms
co-operation 3, 10–16, 25, 27, 38, 116, 130–31
co-ordination 47, 66, 132–3
corporate crime 64–6, 72–7
corporate social responsibility 66–72, 76
corruption 23, 26, 29–33, 38, 45, 53–5
cost-benefit analysis 65
crime 3, 10, 29–33, 55, 57
Crosland, A. 40, 44
Culyer, A. 87
customs 9, 140
   see also conventions, norms
Czech republic 3, 50, 53

Da Re, A. 33, 34
Darwin, C. 110, 118
De George, R. 57, 64, 78
Deane, P. 117, 118
decision theory 7
defection 10–14
Dennison, S. 67, 78
deontology 23, 29–30, 59–60, 65, 146, 148
desert 39
Dettner, J. 78
discrimination 83–6
distribution 32, 101, 111, 147
dominant strategy 124–5, 127
Donaldson, D. 136
Dore, R. 27, 33, 34
Dresler, M. 21
Dunkley, C. 1, 21

Eastern Europe 25–6, 36, 41, 43, 45,
    50–55, 146
economic growth 41–3, 106, 112
efficiency 14, 25–6, 36, 46, 61–3, 71–2,
    81, 101–3, 106, 140, 144, 147
efficiency wages 18
egalitarianism 39–41
egoism *see* self-interest
Eliot, T.S. 96, 100
Elster, J. 149
employment subsidy 51–2
Engels, F. 34
equality 5, 39–40, 83, 86, 98, 146
European social charter 18
Evan, W. 66, 77, 78
exchange 23, 25–6, 32, 47, 102, 106, 117
externalities 28, 60, 70, 128
Exxon Corporation 73–6

fairness 15, 20, 58, 61, 79, 81–3, 85–7,
    98, 101, 145–7
Fein, A. 87
felicity 121–9
Fender, J. 141
Flemming, J. 56, 135, 146
Flood, M. 21
Ford Motor Corporation 64, 73–5
Frank, R. 8, 13, 15–16, 21
freedom 36–7, 38, 41, 43, 59, 61–3, 93,
    131–2, 141, 148
Freeman, R. 60, 66, 77, 78
French, P. 72–3, 78
Fried, C. 87
Friedman, M. 58–9, 64, 78, 111

Gambetta, D. 34
Gauthier, D. 149
generosity 24
Germany 69, 71
Gibbard, A. 149
Gilbert, D. 60, 78
Golden Rule 4–5, 12, 61
Grayson, D. 16, 22
Gregg, C. 100
Griffin, J. 149
Gudex, C. 86, 87

Hahn, F. 107, 118
Haldane, J.B.S. 12
Hamlin, A. 135, 149

Hammond, P. 122, 136
Harcourt, G. 118
Hardin, G. 149
Hare, R. 21
Harrod, R. 90–91, 100
Hausman, D. 22, 136, 149
Hayek, F.A. von 15, 77, 78, 97, 115,
    118, 138, 141, 149
health service 79–87
Hicks, J. 48
Hirschman, A. 149, 150
Hobbes, T. 3
Hobson, J. 149, 150
honesty 9, 13, 29, 43, 58, 127, 142
honour 29–30, 32–3
Hume, D. 2, 5–6, 21, 22, 139, 150

ideal utilitarianism *see* utilitarianism
Ikegami, E. 33, 34
inequality 37, 39–40, 46–7, 60–62, 102,
    138
inflation 50–52, 55, 98, 110
insider dealing 62–3
institutions 7, 9, 15, 26–7, 30–32, 36,
    38, 42, 48–9, 55, 115–17, 120,
    138–48
international economic integration
    101–3, 113–15
invisible hand 2, 8–9, 11, 59, 66, 70,
    104–5, 128, 139–40, 143

Japan 25–8, 33, 35, 69, 71, 78, 116
Jensen, M. 58, 78
Jevons, W. 107
Johnson, H. 5
Johnson & Johnson 65
justice 40–41, 98–9
    the just price 106
    see also equality, fairness

Kaldor, N. 111, 118
Kant, I. 26, 61
Kautilya 30
Kay, J. 4, 22
Keeley, M. 67, 78
Keynes, J.M. 45, 50, 56, 88–100,
    110–12, 118, 146
Keynes, J.N. 90–92, 99, 100
Kirzner, I. 61–2, 78
Klingemann, U. 136

Klitgaard, R. 34
Klouda, P. 87
Knight, F. 62
Kolm, S. 120, 136
Kotlikoff, L. 136
Kranich, L. 136
Kreps, D. 128, 136
Kurz, M. 136

labour market 18–20, 48–51
law 2, 4, 9, 38, 59, 62, 67, 71–7, 140
Lawson, N. 35, 44, 141, 146
Lerner, A. 98–9, 100
liberalization 50–51
liberty *see* freedom
Lindbeck, A. 130, 136
logical positivism 92, 107
Lucas, R. 111
Luther, M. 118

McPherson, M. 22, 136, 149
Mafia 23, 29, 31–3, 45, 53–5
Malthus, T. 106, 110
Mandeville, B. 58–60, 66, 71, 78
Manne, H. 70, 78
Mansbridge, J. 136
market socialism 60
Marshall, A. 89–90, 99, 100, 105, 116
Marx, K. 27–8, 34, 106
Massarenti, A. 33, 34
materialism 6, 13
Matthews, R. 118, 119
Meckling, W. 58, 78
Menger, C. 107
Milgrom, P. 149, 150
Milkin, M. 57
Mill, J.S. 4, 8, 21, 89, 106, 115, 119
Miller, D. 60, 78, 149, 150
Miller, F. 136
minimum wages 18, 51, 109
Mises, L. von 11, 20, 77, 78
monetary policy 49–50
money supply 48
monopoly 48, 54, 68, 108, 147
Monroe, K. 122, 136
Moore, G.E. 4, 88–9, 92–5, 100, 146
moral codes 1–3, 6, 18, 23–34, 37, 89,
    101, 137, 142
Morgan, P. 115
Morishima, M. 27, 34

motivation 7, 14, 24–9, 32, 37–9, 61, 71,
    101, 139–40
    see also self-interest, altruism
multinational enterprises 114–15, 117

Nash equilibrium 124–5, 130
Nash, L. 65, 78
nation state 101–3, 113–16, 147
Nestlé 64–5
Newton, I. 105
Nomura 78
normative economics 1, 89–91, 107,
    120
    see also welfare economics
norms 11, 14, 30–33, 98, 127, 140
    see also conventions, customs
North, D. 149, 150
Nowak, M. 14, 21, 22
Nozick, R. 21, 22

O'Donnell, R. 93, 100
organ transplants 79–80, 82–3, 145
Ornaghi, L. 146

P&O Company 73–6
Panić, M. 118, 119
Pareto, V. 110
Parfit, D. 127–8, 136
Parris, M. 20, 22
Paul, E. 136
Paul, J. 136
Pavarotti, L. 40
Pavlov (in prisoner's dilemma) 14
Peacock, A. 71, 78
Pettit, P. 149
Phelps, E. 136
Phillips curve 50, 110, 112
Plant, R. 41, 44, 149, 150
Plato 30, 92
Pliskin, J. 86, 87
positive economics 1, 90–91, 120
positivism *see* logical positivism
poverty 27, 36, 40–41, 47, 55, 83–5,
    138
power 102
price flexibility 101–19
prisoner's dilemma 8–11, 14–16, 21, 59,
    123–5, 130
private property 2, 35, 38, 46, 94
    see also property rights

privatization 52, 108
production 25–6, 28–9, 32–3, 46, 50–51, 102, 117
profit 11, 16, 53, 61–4, 68, 104
profit-maximization 27–9, 33, 38, 54, 66, 106
property rights 7, 54, 102
  see also private property
public choice 5, 148
public goods 9, 28–9, 33, 47, 59–60, 70, 97, 108, 124, 128
public interest 15
  see also welfare
public spirit 24

quality adjusted life years (qalys) 80–81, 84–6
quasi-market 82

Radnitzky, G. 7, 21, 22
Rapaport, A. 11
rational expectations 49
rationality 7, 13, 65, 71, 88, 91–4, 96, 99, 120–21, 141–3
rationing 79–83, 86
Rawls, J. 96
Razin, A. 136
Reagan, R. 27, 35, 41, 88, 99
reciprocity 11–12, 14, 61
Rees-Mogg, W. 89, 100
Reich, R. 114, 115, 116, 119
Reidenbach, R. 73, 78
Ricardo, D. 106
rights 62, 72, 77, 81, 146–8
Robbins, L. 90–92, 96, 99, 100, 107, 119
Robertson, D. 67, 78, 111, 119
Robin, D. 73, 78
Rosenthal, R. 136
Rothschild, E. 33, 34
rotten kid theorem 133–4
rules 2, 11, 14–16, 26, 31, 59, 93, 102
Russell, B. 3, 20–21, 22, 139
Russia (former Soviet Union) 2–3, 5, 25–6, 50

samaritan's dilemma 129–30
Samuelson, P. 34, 136
Schmoller, G. 107
Schumpeter, J. 36, 44, 70, 99, 100

self-interest 3, 6–14, 23–5, 28, 37–9, 45, 47, 57–9, 61–3, 66, 77, 88, 101–2, 117, 120–21, 125, 129, 141–4
Sen, A. 2, 22, 34, 118, 119, 121, 136, 141, 150
shareholders 4, 17, 58, 62–3, 68–73, 76
Shepard, D. 86, 87
Shove, G. 110
Sigmund, K. 21, 22
Simon, H. 136
Singer, P. 135, 136
Skidelsky, 100, 146
Smith, A. 8–9, 22, 23–6, 32–3, 34, 37, 58, 63, 68, 104–7, 114, 118, 119, 128, 141
Soros, G. 1
Sraffa, P. 106
Stafford, G. 118, 119
stakeholders 69–71
standard of living 5, 27, 35–6, 41–2, 46, 111
Stark, O. 122, 129, 130, 136
Sternberg, E. 16, 22
Stigler, G. 6, 22
Strosberg, M. 87
Sugden, R. 136, 149, 150
Sylos-Labini, P. 118, 119
sympathy 24, 121

takeovers 68, 71
Tawney, R. 28, 34
Temple, W. 89, 99
Texas Gulf Sulpher 63
Thatcher, M. 17, 35, 41, 88, 99
Tinbergen, J. 91
tit-for-tat (in prisoner's dilemma) 11–12, 14
Titmuss, R. 14–15, 125, 136
transition to market economy 45, 53–5, 88, 146
trust 25–7, 32, 43, 47, 116, 142
Tucker, A.W. 21
Tylenol 65

unemployment 18–20, 45, 48–55, 112, 146
universalizability 26
utilitarianism 59–60, 62, 64–5, 76, 93, 122, 146
  ideal utilitarianism 88, 92–4, 146

utility 6–7, 121, 144
utility maximization 12, 91, 121, 141

value judgements 2, 91
    basic and non-basic judgements 2
value pluralism 145, 147
vengeance 15–16, 73
Violante, L. 34
voluntarism 25–6, 43, 60, 141
voting paradox 8, 124

Wade, R. 33, 34
wage flexibility 18–20, 48–52
Waldman, M. 133, 136
Walras, L. 107–8, 110

Walzer, M. 149, 150
Weber, M. 28, 34
Weibull, J. 130, 136
Weingast, B. 149, 150
Weinstein, M. 86, 87
welfare 4, 6, 45–6, 102, 112, 131–2
welfare economics 1, 51, 98, 107–8
    fundamental theorem of welfare
        economics 108, 128–9, 141–2
welfare state 45–7
Werhane, P. 33, 34
Wiener, J. 87
Wilson, C. 115

Zamagni, S. 31